Discover English

Discover English

(A Language Awareness Workbook)

ROD BOLITHO
and
BRIAN TOMLINSON

HEINEMANN EDUCATIONAL BOOKS
London

Heinemann Educational Books Ltd
22 Bedford Square, London WC1B 3HH
LONDON   EDINBURGH   MELBOURNE   AUCKLAND
HONG KONG   SINGAPORE   KUALA LUMPUR
NEW DELHI   IBADAN   NAIROBI   JOHANNESBURG
EXETER (NH)   KINGSTON   PORT OF SPAIN

British Library Cataloguing in Publication Data

Bolitho, Rod
  Discover English
  1. English language – Study and teaching
  – Foreign students
  I. Title   II. Tomlinson, Brian
  428'.2'407   PE1128.A2   80-40773

  ISBN 0 435 28991 8

Typeset in 10 on 11 point Times by V & M Graphics Ltd,
Aylesbury, Bucks
Printed in Great Britain by
Biddles Ltd, Guildford, Surrey

For our families

Acknowledgements

Thanks are due to Ann Campbell for her detailed comments, to Pauline Lea, Dany Donelan and Carole Green for their help in typing the manuscript, to three generations of students on Cambridge RSA Cert T.E.F.L. courses, and to various overseas teachers' groups at Bell College, Saffron Walden with whom we tried the material out and whose comments and reactions helped us greatly.

Contents

..

Introduction

General

This book consists of a collection of exercises written for teachers' pre-service and in-service courses. The purpose of the exercises is to sensitize teachers of English to the language they are teaching, whether they are native teachers taking their first analytical look at their own language or non-native teachers seeking to clarify areas of confusion. It is *not* a language practice book in the conventional sense, though many of the exercises may be found useful by advanced students. Nor is it an attempt at systematic coverage of all points of grammar. It concentrates on exercises on areas which we have identified as problematical for teachers. Too often, teachers master classroom techniques only to fall down on their ability to present language in a correct and clearly thought-out way. This is why many of the exercises examine implications for teaching of discovered facts about language.

There is no particular significance in the order in which the exercises are presented, and they do not constitute a graded course. However, exercises within each unit sometimes depend on each other and a later exercise may refer back to an earlier one.

To the teacher trainer

We have found that teachers need to discover language for themselves, and that 'force-feeding' is an ineffective training technique. This is why none of the exercises has a heading. The index provides a 'way into' the exercises for the teacher trainer, who may like to set exercises as groupwork tasks on his courses; they were written with groupwork in mind and have been tried out in this way. Indeed, most of the exercises are best tackled orally, or answered in note form if set for homework. The commentaries are offered to the teacher trainer as an aid, no more. We have not set out to be prescriptive in the commentaries, and recognise fully that there may be other equally valid versions of many of them. We would expect most experienced native-speaker teacher trainers to dispense completely with the commentaries and simply

1

regard the exercises as source material to be drawn on and used as they see fit. Many of the exercise types used in this book can serve as models for teacher trainers to produce their own exercises on other language problems.

To the teacher, trainee or advanced student using the book privately

Exercises may be selected according to needs, by reference to the index, answers can be jotted down and then checked against the commentaries. These commentaries are intended to provide quick and easy reference. They do not replace a reference grammar. Conclusions are offered with teaching implications constantly in mind, generalisations are made only in order to aid effective teaching and not to establish a set of abstract rules.

We found these reference books useful in writing and revising the material and suggest that those asterisked may prove useful to trainees preparing to teach English for the first time; and to advanced learners.

Meaning and the English verb G. Leech (Longman)

A University Grammar of English R. Quirk et al. (Longman)

A Reference Grammar for Students of English R. A. Close (Longman)

A Communicative Grammar of English G. Leech and J. Svartvik (Longman)

A Grammar of Contemporary English R. Quirk et al. (Longman)

A Practical English Grammar Thompson and Martinet (Oxford University Press)

Practical English Usage M. Swan (Oxford University Press)

EXERCISES

Unit One

SECTION ONE

A.   In the following exercise compare the statement in a) with the evidence in b) and then comment critically on the statement.

1   *a)*   *I want my students to speak only the best English so I encourage them to read only the classics of English literature.*

    b)   i)   *I've tried a long time, and 't'nt got better. But thou'st right; 't might mak fok talk even of thee.*

Hard Times – Charles Dickens

        ii)   *The robbery at the bank had not languished before, and did not cease to occupy a front place in the attention of the Principal of that establishment now.*

Hard Times – Charles Dickens

2   *a)*   'English is a stupid language. It is illogical and irregular and it follows no rules.'

   b)

1	2	3	4
swimming	It's hot, isn't it?	He bought it.	Have you got any money?
dining	She's fat, isn't she?	She grew it.	
sinned	You didn't come, did you?	He brought it.	Have you got some money?
lined	I've won, haven't I?	I showed them.	
hatred	She'll come won't she?	He wanted it.	Give me some books.
baited	He wasn't happy, was he?	I cleaned it.	Give me any books.
getting	The bus is late, isn't it?	I blamed them. He cheated them.	We haven't got any more.
greeting	Mary had finished, hadn't she?	I went there. He sold it.	We haven't got some more.

3   *a)*   'Learning a language is a question of imitating correct forms.'

3

b) i)   *Teacher* – We're having a test today.

           Pupil – Please sir, can I be excused?

                   I'm having a bad headache.

    ii) *Teacher* – Have you ever been to Manchester?

           Pupil – Yes, I've been there last week.

   iii) *Teacher* – When will you do it?

           Pupil – I will do it when I will get home tonight.

B. What contradictions are involved in each of the following statements?

1. 'I will always insist that the pupils who I teach will follow the rules of the language so that they will learn to always speak correctly. I make sure that they always use "shall" with "I", that they always use "whom" when the accusative form is required, that they never split an infinitive and that they never use a preposition to end a sentence with.'

2. 'As I inculcated my amenuensis the sole bonafide mode of indoctrinating a language is to imbibe ten exotic words before retiring to somnambulance each evening. If you do not employ exotic words people deem you to be inerudite in the language.'

C. Comment on the following statements.

1. 'I'm an Englishman and I'm proud of our great and ancient language. We must fight against these modern colloquialisms and the corruption of our language by vulgar Americanisms. Let's keep our language pure.'

2. 'I can understand my teacher very easily but when I talk English to people in the street they speak too quickly.'

3. 'You don't need a teacher to learn a foreign language. All you need is a grammar book and a dictionary.'

4. 'Only speakers of educated, standard southern English should teach English to foreigners. People who speak a dialect teach incorrect English.'

5. 'What's the point of practising the same thing over and over again? I know the conditional tenses.'

6. 'I've been teaching English for thirty years and I know

4

what I'm doing. I teach only what has been judged by time and literature to be correct.'

7. 'I don't think he's a very good teacher. Every time I walk past his classroom the students seem to be sitting in groups making a noise.'

8. 'The use of *hopefully* except with the meaning *in a hopeful way* is unacceptable. So also is the use of *due to* in such public announcements as *Play stopped, due to rain* and *trains delayed, due to ice on the rails.* The phrase should be used only when preceded by a noun or noun plus linking verb, as in *The stoppage was due to rain.*

9. '*Some* is only used in positive statements whereas *any* is used in negative statements and questions.'

10. 'A verb is a doing word.'

11. 'The subject of a sentence is the person or thing that does the action.'

12. 'The past tenses always refer to the past – *e.g. He was going to the match.*'

13. 'Countable nouns refer to things which you can count (*e.g. chairs, books, apples*) whereas uncountable nouns refer to things which you cannot count (*e.g. rice, soap, money*).'

14. 'It's important to insist that learners of a language speak with the same correctness as we would expect when they're writing.'

15. '*will* is never used in clauses which begin with *when, after, before* or *as soon as.*'

16. 'A good English speaker never uses slang so I never allow my students to use English slang.'

Unit Two

SECTION ONE

A. If you can answer these questions, you can leave out the exercises which follow. If not, you will find the exercises useful.

1. What is a noun? Give an example.
2. What is a pronoun? Give an example.
3. What is a transitive verb? Give an example.
4. What is an intransitive verb? Give an example.
5. What is an infinitive? Give an example.
6. Identify (*a*) the subject, (*b*) the main verb and (*c*) the object or complement in each of these examples.
   (*i*)   Churchill smoked cigars.
   (*ii*) Few women smoke cigars.
   (*iii*) Smoking causes health problems.
   (*iv*) Cigarettes are bad for you.
7. What is a preposition? Give an example.
8. What is a conjunction? Give an example.
9. What is an adjective? Give an example.
10. What is an adverb? Give an example.
11. Give an example of a verb with both a direct and an indirect object.

B. Use a dictionary to classify these words into nouns, adjectives, adverbs etc. Subclassify the verbs into transitive and intransitive.

1. window	9. strongly	17. because
2. happiness	10. grin	18. gargoyle
3. meander	11. drink	19. ennui
4. blue	12. iridescent	20. malinger
5. if	13. avoid	21. although
6. under	14. comatose	22. by
7. our	15. courageously	23. aberration
8. be	16. cogitate	24. fabricate

C. Look at the verbs in these utterances and divide them into two categories, stating reasons for your allocation.
1. 'You've finished your tea.'
2. 'They are eating cake.'
3. 'They are eating at home.'
4. 'She wants to watch T.V.'
5. 'I'm going to bed.'
6. 'I'm repairing the car.'
7. Hillary and Tenzing conquered Everest.
8. Churchill died several years ago.
9. 'I can't think clearly!'
10. 'I hate this exercise!'

D. What is the direct object in each of these sentences?
1. He took his girlfriend to the cinema last night.
2. Afterwards, he took her out for a meal.
3. He bought her champagne.
4. After the meal he drove her home.
5. He kissed her on the doorstep.
6. She asked him in for a nightcap.
7. She closed the curtains and made the coffee.
8. He made an excuse, got up and went home.

E. Why are these utterances wrong?
1. He got up early because his work.
2. He gave she a present.
3. They ate a quickly breakfast before going out.
4. During they were eating, the doorbell rang.
5. 'There's something blocking the road.' 'O.K., we'll avoid.'
6. He learns very slow.
7. They gives her a lot of help.
8. 'I want to listen the news at 9 o'clock.'

F. Why do these nonsense sentences **sound** acceptable?
1. He crattled his splod and scrot out a neelying groal.
2. They strentered folicly until a magan veened to famble them.

7

G. Look these words up in a dictionary.

sits	was	swore	swam
spoken	bought	sung	knocked
talked	driven	drew	burnt.

How does the dictionary deal with them?

SECTION TWO

Look at these groups of utterances. What do the utterances in each group have in common? What distinguishes them? If necessary, check in the commentary after doing exercise **A** to see whether you are on the right track.

A.
1. Willy smokes
2. Fred's a slow worker.
3. Aggie used to drink.
4. Joe's in the habit of talking in his sleep.
5. He's always making that mistake.

B.
1. Pollution is getting worse.
2. It's raining.
3. I'm going out tonight.
4. He's always dropping ash on the carpet.

C.
1. Simmer for 15 minutes over a low heat.
2. Come again soon.
3. Halt!
4. Give us this day our daily bread.
5. Don't mention it.
6. When in Rome, do as the Romans do.

D.
1. See you!
2. The Queen is due to arrive at 4 p.m.
3. He's about to arrive.
4. The train leaves at 3 p.m.
5. Willy's going to be an engine driver.
6. He's taking his finals in June.
7. I'll be 64 next birthday.

E.
1. If I were you, I'd stay.
2. It's time you went home.
3. Wish you were here!
4. If only he had worked harder!
5. Suppose someone had seen us.

8

F.   1. I doubt if he'll come.
   2. It might rain.
   3. There's a 50-50 chance of play today.
   4. He's bound to turn up.
   5. She's likely to pass her test.

SECTION THREE

A.   Look at this diagram representing time.

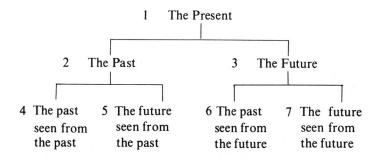

Allocate the utterances below to numbers on the diagram.
(*i*)   We're going to live in Liverpool.
(*ii*)   After we've lived in Liverpool for a few years, we'll move back to Wigan.
(*iii*)   We live in Wigan.
(*iv*)   We lived in Bradford for 5 years.
(*v*)   We were going to move to London in 1973 but my job there fell through.
(*vi*)   By the time we move to Liverpool, we'll have spent 3 years in Wigan.
(*vii*)   We lived in Manchester for a while before we moved to Bradford.
Find other ways of expressing the same ideas.

B.   Comment on the validity of these statements:
   1. Present tenses are always used to express present time.
   2. Past tenses are always used to express past time.

3. The English tense system is based on, and can be equated with, the Latin tense system.
4. Different peoples perceive time differently, and these differences are reflected in the tense systems of their languages.
5. Different languages have developed different ways of referring to commonly perceived concepts of time.
6. The verb is the main marker of time in an English sentence.

SECTION FOUR

A. Divide these questions into two broad categories; state what your criteria are.
   1. Where's my pen?
   2. When is the train due in?
   3. Are you listening?
   4. How far is it to London?
   5. Isn't that my pen?
   6. Why haven't you done your homework?
   7. That's not your pen, is it?
   8. Would you like coffee or tea?
   9. Would like some more wine?
   10. What's the time?
   11. You've been to Liverpool before, haven't you?
   12. How are you?

B. Divide these questions into categories; state what your criteria are.
   1. Is the T.V. still on?.
   2. Haven't you finished eating yet?
   3. Can you lend me £5?
   4. That's not Helen, is it?
   5. Have you locked the back door?
   6. Has someone opened this letter?
   7. It isn't raining again, is it?
   8. Do you mind if I smoke?
   9. Was Mike at the party last night?

10. Shall I open the door for you?
11. This can't possibly be right, can it?
12. Do you want some more cake?
13. You have posted the letter, haven't you?
14. Nice day, isn't it?

C. Account for these foreign students' errors in question formation.
   1.x Does he plays tennis?
   2.x Am not I right?
   3.x Did you went to town last week?
   4.x How often play you tennis?
   5.x Do you can play chess?
   6.x You don't like carrots, like you?
   7.x Shall you open the door for me, please?

D. Look at these sets of questions and answers and explain the misunderstandings.
   1. *a:* How do you do?
      b: I do very well, thank you.
   2. *a:* How are you?
      b: How are you?
   3. *a:* Can you open the door?
      b: (*not moving*) Yes, I can.
   4. *a:* Do you read a newspaper?
      b: No, I have my tea.
   5. *a:* You've finished that work, haven't you?
      b: (*impatiently*) Of course I have.

E. Look at these questions and at the list of functions below. Decide on a function for each question.

QUESTIONS
   1. What time is it?
   2. Is that a stoat or a weasel?
   3. You're back rather early, aren't you?
   4. What do you mean *early*?
   5. *Must* you play your harmonica in the living-room?
   6. Shall I do that for you?

11

7. Would you mind holding this for a moment?
8. Why are you late?
9. What sort of car was he driving?
10. What do you think of the new centre-forward?

FUNCTIONS
a) asking someone to distinguish between alternatives
b) expressing incredulity
c) offering assistance
d) asking for assistance
e) asking for information
f) expressing irritation
g) asking for an opinion
h) expressing mild surprise
i) asking for an explanation
j) asking for a description

F. Food for thought.
　　1. Why do you think foreign learners are often very bad at forming and asking questions?
　　2. In the light of your conclusions after the preceding exercises, why do you think it is important for a language teacher to distinguish between the terms *question* and *interrogative*?

SECTION FIVE

A. In many grammars and coursebooks, the future is dealt with as a tense, formed by *shall/will* + infinitive. It is often known as the **pure future**. Which of the following examples could be described as **pure future**? What do *shall* or *will* add to the meaning in the other examples?
　　1. 'Don't worry! I'll help you with your homework.'
　　2. My brother **will** talk with his mouth full.
　　3. 'Pass the mustard, will you?'
　　4. 'Shall I open the door for you?'
　　5. 'I'll see you at the party tonight.'
　　6. 'Shall we go for a drink?'

7. Trespassers will be prosecuted.
8. Boys will be boys.
9. 'Do you think Liverpool will win?'
10. 'You shall do as I tell you!'
11. Summer will soon be over.

B. Look at these different ways of expressing future meaning and comment on why you think there is no standardised future **tense** in English.
1. She'll be 83 next July.
2. 'I'm just going down to the village.'
   'Will you be going near the Post Office?'
3. 'I've lost my wallet again!'
   'What are you going to do about it?'
4. 'There's going to be a crash on that bend soon.'
5. 'What are you doing this evening?'
6. 'We hope to go abroad next year.'
7. John is about to resign from his job.
8. You never know what might happen.
9. The film starts at 8.15.

C. Which way of expressing the future would you teach first. Why?

D. Which of these statements about *shall* and *will* do you accept?
1. *Shall* is never used these days.
2. *Shall* ought always to be used with the first person and *will* with the second and third persons.
3. In conversation, the difference between *shall* and *will* has become unimportant (in most cases).
4. *Shall* ought always to be taught as it is strictly correct in certain cases.
5. There is no real need to teach *shall*.
How many of the statements could also apply to *should* and *would*?

SECTION SIX

A. Comment on the form of these statements. Where might they be found?

    1. On parle français.   2. Se habla español.

    3. Man spricht Deutsch.   4. English spoken.

B. What might be the contexts of the following short extracts? Give reasons for your conclusions.

    1. Customers are asked to use the baskets provided.

    2. My car's been stolen!

    3. 200 people are reported to have died in the riots.

    4. It's being repaired.

    5. You have been warned!

    6. Trespassers will be prosecuted.

    7. Kennedy assassinated.

C. What is wrong with this passage? Improve it.

Oxygen

Joseph Priestley prepared oxygen for the first time in 1774. He prepared it by heating mercuric oxide, but nowadays we produce it commercially in large quantities by a process which we call fractional distillation. Both air and water contain it. Plants also give it off in their respiratory process.

D. Comment on this exercise.

Make these sentences passive.

Example: *John wrote that letter*

              That letter was written by John

    1. The cow jumped over the moon.

    2. Willy ate his sister's porridge.

    3. Shakespeare wrote *Hamlet.*

    4. Somebody broke into our house last night.

    5. Koala bears eat eucalyptus leaves.

    6. The Queen has just opened Parliament.

E. Compare the effect of active vs passive in these utterances.

    1. They went home as there was nothing more to do.

       They went home as there was nothing more to be done.

2. There's nothing to see in Scotland.
   There was no-one to be seen on the streets.

F. What have these sentences in common?
   1. I was born in 1944.
   2. He is reputed to be rich.
   3. Smoking is forbidden in here.
   4. You are not obliged to help.

G. What is the effect of the use of the passive in these mini-dialogues?
   1. *Soldier*: Sorry I'm late, sir. It wasn't my fault.
      Officer: You've been warned about lateness before.
      Soldier: I know, sir.
   2. *Interviewer*: Can you give an undertaking to keep inflation down?
      Prime Minister: It is to be hoped that it will not exceed 10% this year.
   3. *Interviewer*: And where is the General now?
      Spokesman: He is believed to be abroad.
   4. *Professor*: Have you read *Look Back in Anger*?
      Student: No, but I've read some of Braine's other books.
      Professor: But *Look Back in Anger* was written by John Osborne.
   5. *Willy*: What's happened to Joe?
      Fred: He's been taken to hospital.

H. Why is the passive so common
   1. in newspaper headlines?
   2. in politicians' speeches?
   3. in scientific reports?
   ... and so uncommon in normal colloquial English?

I. Compare these pairs of sentences:
   1. He's just had his watch repaired.
      He's just repaired his watch.
   2. Where can I get this film developed?
      Where can this film be developed?
   3. He's just had three teeth out.
      Three of his teeth have just been taken out.

J. Try this exercise and comment on its effectiveness.
COMPLETE EACH SENTENCE ON THE LINES OF THE EXAMPLE
Do you repair your own car or *do you have it repaired*?
1. Do you cut your own hair or ....
2. Do you do your own gardening or ....
3. Do you fetch your own newspaper or.............................
4. Do you make your dresses yourself or............................
5. Do you clean your car yourself or ....

SECTION SEVEN

A. Comment on the verb forms in **heavy** type in these utterances. Are they past tenses?
1. If only it **would rain**!
2. If only it **rained** more often!
3. I wish you **were** here.
4. If I **were** a rich man, I wouldn't have to work hard.
5. If I **had** a hammer, I'd hammer in the morning.
6. It's time you **washed** your feet.
7. Suppose you **were** in my position, what would you do?
8. '**Had** you **arrived** earlier, you'd have had enough to drink.'
9. He speaks as if he **knew** everything about cars.
10. 'Would you mind if I **smoked**?'

B. Which of these utterances might apply to (*a*) a good student, (*b*) a lazy student and (*c*) an ex-student?
1. If he worked hard, he'd pass.
2. If he had worked hard, he'd've passed.
3. He'll pass if he works hard.

C. Group these utterances according to the function of *would* in each.
1. 'He told me he would pay me back.'
2. 'I wish it would rain.'
3. 'Would you mind helping me?'
4. It would be difficult to refuse such an offer if it came.

16

5. 'I've forgotten my keys.'
   'You would!'
6. 'You would do well to take his advice!'
7. Queen Victoria would seldom smile.
8. 'I'd be grateful if you would stop blowing smoke in my eyes.'
9. 'I was hoping you would come.'
10. 'Would that you were here!'

In the light of your observations, do you think it is useful to talk about a conditional **tense?** or about conditional **sentences?**

D. Place these utterances into **three** groups for teaching purposes. State your criteria.
1. 'I wish I had more time.'
2. 'If you come tonight, you'll meet her.'
3. 'If only I had worked harder!'
4. 'You'll have an accident unless you slow down.'
5. 'I'd take care if I were you.'
6. 'There'll be no trouble provided you keep calm.'
7. 'You'd do well to cut down your smoking.'
8. There might never have been an accident if the road had been dry.
9. 'I'd feel better if I could lie down.'
10. Without the millions invested by the oil companies, North Sea oil might never have been discovered.
11. 'Given a little luck, we'll succeed.'
12. 'Should you change your mind, I'll be happy to hear from you.'
13. 'Were you to have second thoughts, I'd be glad to re-open negotiations.'

SECTION EIGHT

A. What are the possible functions of each of the words or phrases in **heavy** type?
1. **I have given** it to him.
2. *a)* **How about** using glue? *b)* **Let's go.**

3. The water **was heated** to a temperature of 80°C.
4. You are coming tonight, **aren't you?**
5. I showed him the book **so that he could** help me to solve the problem.
6. **Do you think you could find time** to look through this book?
7. He walked to the window **and** opened it as far as it would go.
8. I **meet** him next Tuesday.
9. It's not something I've had much experience in. **Nevertheless** I'll do it for you.
10. **The** house is for sale now.
11. **It's not only** the cost that is the problem; I just haven't got time.
12. **It** has been discussed many times before.
13. I **rang** him yesterday at ten.
14. He is **always** picking his nose.
15. He bought two books **and** three magazines.
16. **I'm not entirely sure that I agree.**

B. What is meant by *function* in **A**?

C. Look back at the fifteen examples in A and use them to help you to write different definitions of the term *function*. Then place each example with one of your definitions.

D. What do you think is meant by *'function'* in *'We must teach both the form and the function of structures'*?

E. What is meant by *'functional'* in *'The Functional Approach puts the emphasis on what is done through language'*?

F. What is the function of each of the expressions in **heavy** type in the following sentences?
1. *A* **Let's go** now.
   B **No way.**
2. *A* **I'm sure** their offer is a very fair one.
   B **No way.**
3. *A* **Would you like to** come in for a coffee?
   B **Thank you very much.**

18

4. *A* **Press** button A.

   B **Again**?

5. *A* You **ought to** get out more.

   B **Too true**.

SECTION NINE

A. Look at the following utterances.
1. I'm not quite sure I agree.
2. You could be right but I think . . .
3. That's your opinion, is it?
4. I would like to contest that point.
5. I disagree.
6. I don't think it's right . . .
7. I'm not so sure I would go along with you there.
8. Nonsense!
9. That's not true.
10. I'd like to express my disagreement . . .
11. That's all very well but . . .
12. On the contrary . . .
13. No way.
14. Balls!
15. I don't think I agree . . .

1. What do all the above utterances have in common?
2. Make generalisations about the differences between the above utterances.
3. If you were going to teach the function of disagreement to a group of post-elementary adult learners which of the above utterances would you teach? How would you teach them?
4. List other exponents of the function of disagreement. Would you teach any of these to the group specified in 3 above?
5. What conclusions can you draw from the questions 1-4 above about the teaching of functions?

B. Two students performed the following impromptu dialogue after being taught ways of complaining and apologising.

    A: Excuse me, would you mind turning down your radio?

    B: Oh, I am terribly sorry. What can I possibly do to put it right?

    A: I won't ask you again.

    B: Not at all. I really must apologise.

    A: I must warn you I won't tolerate it any more.

    B: I'm so sorry.

    1.   What is wrong with the dialogue?

    2.   What faults in the teaching do you think might have been responsible for the students' producing such a faulty performance?

    3.   As a result of your analysis of this dialogue what would you say were the most important things to remember when teaching functions?

C. 1.   What is wrong with the following dialogue?

        A: Please could you possibly lend me £5?

        B: I'm broke.

        A: How about lending me your car?

        B: I wish I could but it's in the garage.

        A: I'd be so grateful if you could find your way to lending me your pen for a minute.

        B: No way.

        A: Give me a cigarette.

        B: If only I could.

    2.   What two functions are exemplified in the above dialogue?

    3.   What are the differences between the exponents of each of the two functions exemplified in the dialogue?

    4.   List other exponents of the two functions and try to place them in categories.

    5.   Select exponents of the two functions to teach to a lower intermediate class. For each exponent say what you think it would be important for the learner to learn about it.

SECTION TEN

A. Look at this utterance and decide how many of the functions below it can realise, according to situation:
Take your watch off before you jump in, she said.

ordering	cajoling	begging	reminding
inviting	persuading	advising	insisting
requesting	permitting	recommending	suggesting
warning	compelling	intending	approving.
threatening	scolding		

B. Now turn the same utterance into indirect speech, once for each of the functions you have chosen.

C. Comment on this exercise for foreign learners.
PUT THE FOLLOWING INTO REPORTED SPEECH:
   1. 'Go to your room and stay there till I call you!' he said.
   2. 'Finish your meat or there'll be no ice-cream,' she said.
   3. 'Don't spend all your money in one shop,' he said.
   4. 'Keep still,' he said, irritably.
   5. 'Wait here till the taxi arrives,' she said.
   6. 'Don't you dare run away again!' he said.
   7. 'Don't shoot, please,' he said in a quavering voice.
   8. 'Take your partners for the rhumba,' the bandleader said.
   9. 'Listen to me, will you,' said the teacher curtly.
   10. 'Lead us not into temptation . . .' (The Lord's Prayer).

SECTION ELEVEN

A. 1. What do the expressions in **heavy** type in the following sentences have in common?
   1. I'm going **for a** month.
   2. He's lived here **since** 1972.
   3. We waited **till** ten.
   4. Stay here **until** I come back.
   5. We had to wait **a long time.**
   6. He **was watching** television.

     7.   We **had been waiting** for three hours when he arrived.

     8.   **How long** did you stay there?

     9.   We enjoyed **the day** immensely.

   10.   We spent **a week** there.

   11.   I **think** he's an honest man.

2.   Make generalisations about when each of the expressions could be used.

   e.g. 2.   To refer to a period of time in the past from the date mentioned to a point of time established by the situation (i.e. now) or a previous utterance. Always followed by an expression referring to a point of time.

3.   Write down any other similar expressions you can think of and then either link them to generalisations you have already made or, if this is not possible, make separate generalisations about them.

B.   1.   What do the expressions in **heavy** type have in common?

     1.   The lorry **moved slowly forward.**

     2.   He has **gone to** Wigan.

     3.   I just saw him **going into** that pub.

     4.   He was **walking towards** Linton.

     5.   He's **gone out.**

     6.   He **ran away from** the fire.

     7.   **Go** and **fetch** it.

   2.   Make generalisations about the use of the underlined expressions.

   3.   Write down any similar expressions you can think of and then make generalisations about them.

   4.   Decide what aspects of the notion of movement you would teach to an elementary class and then for each aspect decide which actual expressions you would teach.

C.   1.   The following expressions can be used to communicate the notion of location.

here	where
there	somewhere
inside	everywhere

outside   on

this   in

that

Use *inside*, *this* and *on* in sentences in which they communicate the notion of location.

2. What notion can all of the following expressions communicate?

    next to   in front of

    between   beside

    behind   on top of

3. What notion can all of the following expressions communicate?

    first   afterwards

    then   later on

    had left   before

D. 1. What notions do each of the expressions in **heavy** type communicate?

    1. Do it **like this**.

    2. He ate so much **that he felt ill**.

    3. It's **not the same thing**.

    4. You can open the door **with** this key.

    5. **At the same time** the bomb went off.

2. For each notion that you have referred to in 1, list three other exponents (i.e. expressions which can communicate aspects of the notion) and comment on the differences (if any) between the three exponents.

E. You have decided to teach the notion of contrast to an intermediate level class.

    1. Which expressions/structures would you teach? Why?

    2. Which order would you teach them in? Why?

    3. Would you teach them together in the same teaching unit or separately? Why?

    4. How would you teach them?

F. Do you think it is a good idea to devise teaching units in which you teach different expressions/structures which can be used to communicate aspects of the same notion? Give reasons for your opinion.

SECTION TWELVE

A. Sort these sentences into two categories: (*a*) those in which the verb in **heavy** type is the main verb and (*b*) those in which the meaning of the verb is *modified* in some way.

1. Children **are** noisy.
2. The T.V. **is** broken.
3. The T.V. must **be** broken.
4. 'I **see** my doctor every Monday.'
5. 'You ought to **see** him more often.'
6. 'I'm afraid I can't **see** him any more often.'
7. 'Joe **was** in London yesterday.'
8. 'But he couldn't **have been**.'
9. 'Why not?' 'Because I **saw** him in Liverpool.'
10. He'll **be** 64 next birthday.
11. 'Will you **open** the door for me?'
12. 'You'll have to **work**.'
13. 'Do you think John is likely **to come?**'
14. 'I think he might **come**.'
15. 'But it's essential that he should **come**.'

In what different ways are the meanings of the verbs in category (*b*) modified?

B. We often speak of degrees of likelihood in terms of percentages. Look at this simplified diagram:

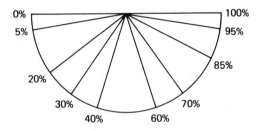

If 0% = *out of the question*, and 100% = *absolute certainty*, allocate these statements to segments of the chart which you feel indicate correctly the degree of likelihood which they express.

1. Willy is definitely in England.
2. Willy may be in England.
3. There's an even chance that Willy's in England.
4. Willy might be in England.
5. There's no way that Willy could be in England.
6. Willy's probably in England.
7. Willy must be in England.
8. Willy just might be in England.
9. I doubt if Willy's in England.
10. Willy may very well be in England.
11. Willy could be in England.
12. Willy is likely to be in England.
13. Perhaps Willy's in England.
14. Willy's almost certainly in England.
15. Willy ought to be in England.

Which of these sentences would you teach first? Why?

C. Look at these different ways of asking for permission. What distinguishes them?
1. 'OK if I go home now?'
2. 'Would you mind if I went home now?'
3. 'Can I go home now?'
4. 'May I go home now?'
5. 'Do you think I might go home now?'
6. 'Could I go home now?'

Which of these would you teach first? Why?

D. Explain the function of the words in **heavy** type in each utterance.
1. It **may** rain this afternoon.
2. Willy **could** run fast when he was a boy.
3. '**May** I ask a question?'
4. 'You **needn't** go if you don't want to.'
5. 'You **might have** told me you were coming.'
6. 'That **can't** be true!'
7. 'They **must** be away. The curtains are drawn.'
8. He was told he **could** re-sit the exam.
9. 'I've failed!' 'You **could** try again next year.'
10. 'I **must** go.'

25

E.   Jot down as many different ways as you can of:
1. expressing possibility
2. expressing ability
3. imposing obligations on others
4. expressing necessity
5. expressing annoyance at irritating habits.

F.   What is the difference (if any) between:
1. *could* and *was able*
2. *mustn't* and *don't have to*
3. *should* and *ought to*
4. *needn't* and *don't need to*
5. '*I may* come' and '*I might* come'
6. *modal auxiliaries* and '*ordinary' auxiliaries*
7. *shall* and *will*
8. *used to* and *would*

SECTION THIRTEEN

A.   What is the main difference in function between the verbs underlined once and the verbs underlined twice in the following sentences?
1. He has gone to the cinema.
2. I must get some work done.
3. No, I didn't see him at the match.
4. Have you met him before?
5. I was waiting for him to come.
6. I can see him now.
7. I am working tonight. I'll ring you tomorrow.

B.   What is the difference in function between the verbs underlined once and the verbs underlined twice in the following sentences?
1. I am English.
2. I am going there tonight.
3. He has four sisters.
4. He has gone to bed.
5. He does two hours homework every night.
6. Does he like children?

26

C. 1. What are the similarities and the differences in function between the verbs underlined once and the verbs underlined twice in the following sentences?

      1. <u><u>Can</u></u> you swim?.
      2. <u><u>Did</u></u> you swim?
      3. You <u>must</u> go, <u><u>mustn't</u></u> you?
      4. You <u>are</u> going, <u><u>aren't</u></u> you?
      5. <u><u>Has</u></u> the milkman been yet? Yes, he <u>has</u>.
      6. You <u>ought</u> to go home now.
      7. <u><u>Shall I tell</u></u> him?
      8. <u><u>He doesn't</u></u> want to come.
      9. They <u>had</u> already finished.
      10. He <u><u>couldn't</u></u> do it.
           No, he <u><u>couldn't</u></u>.

    2. List other verbs like those underlined twice.

D. What are the differences in function between the three verbs in the following sentence?

He **has had to have** an operation.

E. The verbs in **heavy** type in the following utterances are all auxiliary verbs. Make generalisations about the functions of this type of verb after examining the following utterances.

    1. **Did** you like him?
       Yes, I **did**.
    2. I **don't** like chips.
       Don't you?
    3. They **haven't** even started yet.
    4. You've lost it, **haven't** you?
    5. He **is** doing it tonight.
    6. **Had** he already mentioned it to you?
    7. They **are** coming, **aren't** they?
    8. **Are** you listening?
       Yes, I **am**.
    9. He **was** hoping to go to university, **wasn't** he?
    10. **Haven't** they gone to Brighton?
       No. But they **did** last year though.

F. 1. Fill in the blanks in the dialogue below with verbs.

     Roy: ___ she wearing that seductive red dress last night?
        ₁

Sam: No, she ___. She ___ bought a black one which
              2   3
   ___ even more seductive.
    4

Roy: ___ you dance with her?
    5

Sam: Yes, I ___. Two or three times. But then so ___
           6   7
   every other man at the party.

Roy: ___ there any other attractive women at the party?
    8

Sam: Yes, lots. But none of them ___ what Mary has.
                            9

Roy: I ___ hoping to take her to the dance like I ___ last
       10   11
   year but she ___ already agreed to go with Ian.
              12

2. For each blank that you have filled in the dialogue above say whether the verb is an auxiliary verb or not. If it is an auxiliary verb, describe its function.

SECTION FOURTEEN

A. Ask the questions which might have prompted these answers. Use *have* in each question, except those marked with an asterisk. What conclusions do you draw from the exercise?

*1. 'It rang when I was having a bath.'
*2. 'I was having a bath when it rang.'
 3. 'No, I'm sorry, I haven't.'
 4. 'Yes, I did.'
 5. 'No, he hasn't, he's got three.'
 6. 'I had a boiled egg, two slices of toast and a cup of tea.'
 7. 'An Opel Kadett.'
*8. 'I'm having a sit-down and a smoke.'
 9. 'No, never.'
10. 'Yes, I'll be having one next month.'
11. 'A boy.'
12. 'Sorry, I don't carry matches.'

B. Comment on the meanings of *be* and *have* in these utterances.

 1. He is having his tonsils out tomorrow.

2. Don't be cruel.
3. He has three cooked meals a day.
4. She's just being stupid.
5. Have a drink on me.
6. She's just had her hair permed.
7. Our house is being repainted.

C. One of each of the following pairs of utterances is wrong or at least unlikely. Identify it and say why you think it is wrong or unlikely.

1. (a) Be careful!
   (b) Be handsome!
2. (a) Don't be late!
   (b) He's being late.
3. (a) She's being stubborn.
   (b) She's being beautiful.
4. (a) I'm having three sisters.
   (b) I'm having a bath.
5. (a) Have a cigarette!
   (b) Have a headache!
6. (a) We've just had tea.
   (b) We've just had a new car.
7. (a) Being British, we were readily accepted.
   (b) We're being French.
8. (a) She's got a brand new coat.
   (b) She's got her dinner at 8.30 every evening.
9. (a) I don't have coffee every day.
   (b) I don't always be stupid.

D. Divide these utterances into two categories according to how **have** and **be** are used.

1. He **has** a cup of tea every morning.
2. He **has** a cup of tea in his hand.
3. 'Her cat's just **had** kittens.'
4. 'You**'re** stupid.'
5. They **have** three children.
6. '**Being** stupid, you wouldn't understand.'
7. Walls **have** ears.
8. 'You're **being** stupid!'
9. 'Can I **have** a look, please?
10. '**Have** a good time!'

11. '**Be** a good boy!'
12. '**Have** a piece of chewing gum.'
13. 'We **haven't** any apples.'
14. He's a careful driver.

E. In which of these utterances do **be** and **have** function as auxiliaries?
   1. He **was** born in 1940.
   2. **Having** seen *The Mousetrap*, I don't know why it's so popular.
   3. He's[1] just **been**[2] to London.
   4. **Being** bright, he understood.
   5. Our car's[1] **being**[2] repaired.
   6. 'Do you always **have** a shower before breakfast?'
   7. '**Have**[1] you **had**[2] lunch yet?'
   8. He told her to **be** sensible.
   9. 'What **have** you got in your hand?'
   10. 'Don't **be** obstructive!'

F. 1. 'We shouldn't teach *have got* (e.g. *She's got one*) as it's too colloquial.' Discuss.
   2. How did this mistake arise? *A. Don't be silly!*
                                 B. (foreign learner) *I don't!*
   3. And this one? *A. Where are my keys?*
                   B. (foreign learner) *I haven't them.*
   4. What are the implications of these exercises for the teaching of *be* and *have* to foreign learners?

SECTION FIFTEEN

A. What do the following utterances have in common? What distinguishes them?
   1. The Nile is longer than the Zambesi.
   2. The Volkswagen has its engine at the back whereas the Mini has it under the bonnet.
   3. Black coal is usually found a long way below the earth's surface; brown coal, on the other hand, is found on the surface.

4. Willy is not as bright as his brother.
5. Maggie didn't like the flat she was living in. She moved to a different one.
6. His hair is the same colour as mine.
7. 'I wish you'd speak more clearly!'
8. He's less of an extrovert than his brother.
9. More motorists are in the *AA* than any other motoring organisation.
10. 'I eat more than I should.'
11. 'I hope you'll be as happy as we are.'
12. The more, the merrier.
13. 'It's as cold as ice out there.'
14. 'You can't do better than your best.'

B. The following is a textbook exercise on comparatives and superlatives.
(a) What does it practise and what does it leave out?
CHOOSE THE CORRECT COMPARATIVE OR SUPERLATIVE FORM OF ONE OF THESE ADJECTIVES OR ADVERBS TO COMPLETE EACH SENTENCE:

fast   far   difficult   high   old   heavy
beautiful   careful   obedient   bad

1. An elephant is . . . . . than a hippopotamus.
2. Chinese is a . . . . . language to learn than Spanish.
3. Henry drives . . . . . than his brother.
4. Henry is . . . . . than his brother.
5. 'Drive . . . . . or we'll be late.'
6. Dogs are generally . . . . . than cats.
7. Mont Blanc is the . . . . . peak in the Alps.
8. Many people think that Paris is the . . . . . city in the world.
9. It is . . . . . from London to Edinburgh than from London to Brussels!
10. His condition is gradually getting . . . . .

(b) What *rules* useful to foreign learners can be generalised from these examples?

31

SECTION SIXTEEN

A. Write down the verbs in each of the following utterances. For each verb name its tense and describe the function(s) of the tense in the utterance.

1. When they got to the station the train had already gone.
2. I was walking along Church St when I saw Mary.
3. The programme will have finished by the time you have finished making the coffee.
4. You're too late. He's just gone home.
5. I see Bill got arrested again yesterday.
6. He walked to work every day when he worked at the station in 1968.
7. When he comes I will let you know.
8. *Passenger*: Which platform does the London train leave from?
    Porter (pointing to a train): It's just gone.
9. I've been waiting here for thirty minutes.
10. I meet him tomorrow at ten o'clock.
11. Has he come yet?

B. Answer the following questions on the utterances in **A** above.

1. In 1 how do we know that the train left before they got to the station?
2. How would substituting *walked* for *was walking* change the meaning of 2?
3. a) Why is the verb in the second clause of 3 in a different tense from the verb in the first clause?
    b) Would changing the form of the second verb to *will have finished making* change the meaning of the sentence?
    c) Would changing the form of the first verb to *has finished* alter the meaning of the sentence?
4. Is the choice of tense in the second sentence of 4 crucial to the meaning of the sentence? Why?
5. Could the verbs in 5 be put into other tenses without seriously affecting the meaning of the sentence?
6. How important is the choice of tense in the first clause of 6 in indicating **past habit**?

32

7. Does the choice of tense in *when he comes* contribute to the meaning of the sentence in 7?

8. In 8 does the porter's choice of tense contribute significantly to the meaning of his utterance?

9. Could any other tense be used in 9 without changing the meaning of the sentence?

10. a) What does the choice of tense in 10 tell us which we could not have deduced from the other elements in the sentence?

   b) What does it tell us which is also communicated by other elements in the sentence?

11. How important is the choice of tense to the meaning of sentence 11?

C. The following incomplete statements are based on an analysis of the utterances in **A** above. Fill in the blanks to complete them.

1. In some utterances the choice of tense is crucial as the use of a different tense would ___ ___ ___ of the utterance.

2. In some utterances the choice of tense is not absolutely crucial as the _____ which it has been chosen to communicate is also communicated by ___ ___ in the utterance and/or by . . . .

3. In some utterances the tense does not contribute significantly to the . . . . as other elements of the ____ and the _____ make the _____ absolutely _____. In such utterances the tense is chosen mainly for its _____ rather than for the _____ that it can convey and an error in the choice of tense would not necessarily . . . .

D. Check your answers to **C** above in the commentary on this unit and then complete the following table by putting each verb from the utterances in **A** in the appropriate column.

N.B.

The numbers at the head of the columns refer to the statements in **C** above.

1	2	3
was walking (2)	got (1)	
	had gone (1)	

E. Write two examples of your own in which the choice of verb tense is crucial to the meaning of the utterance.

F. Write two examples of your own in which the choice of verb tense reinforces the function of another element in the utterance.

G. Write two examples of your own in which the verb tense is appropriate but is not crucial because other elements of the utterance of the situation communicate the same function.

H. Complete the analysis of tense significance below the following passage.

The old woman had been moved into the small room where the child had slept and the man with the red moustache had been shifted into what the nurse now called the convalescence room. In the middle room Jennifer lay with her eyes closed. They had apparently succeeded in removing the book as it was lying face down on the table.

Analysis

1. **had been moved** – the selection of the past perfect tense is crucial as it is the only indicator that the moving had been completed before the arrival of the writer.
2. **had slept** – the selection ....
3. ....

I. Analyse the tense significance of the verbs in the dialogue below:

Mary: Here it is. It's been in this cupboard all the time we've been looking for it.

Simon: Good. I'll take it to the pub tonight. I'm meeting Arthur at nine; I'll give it to him then. I was going to buy him another one.

Mary: The phone's ringing.

34

Simon: I'll get it. Sam usually rings about this time.
Mary: It's stopped ringing. You didn't answer it quickly enough.

J. What is the relevance of this unit to the teaching of the tenses of English?

SECTION SEVENTEEN

A. Sort these utterances into 2 categories. Say what your categories are.
1. Fred went to London last week.
2. 'I was working for a cigarette company in May last year.'
3. He's just having dinner.
4. 'I'll be at the meeting tomorrow.'
5. Maggie goes fishing on Sundays.
6. 'I'll be lying on the beach at Torremolinos this time next week.'

B. Account for these wrong utterances by foreign learners:
1. *Q*: What did you do when the telephone rang?
   A(F.L.): I wrote a letter.
2. *Q*: Cigarette?
   A(F.L): No thanks. I'm not smoking.
3. *Q*: What do you think of the government?
   A(F.L): I'm liking it very much.
4. *Q(F.L)*: Where are you going?
   A: To town.
   Q: Will you go to the post office?
5. *Q*: What were you doing when the doorbell rang?
   A(F.L): I got up and opened the door.
6. *Q(F.L)*: Where have you been last night?
7. *Q*: Who built that wall?
   A(F.L): The Romans had built it 2,000 years ago.

C. In view of these typical and frequent errors, how do you think foreign learners can be helped to understand the difference between tense and aspect?

SECTION EIGHTEEN

A. Comment on these statements about usage:
1. The simple past is always used for completed actions.
2. The most common use of the present continuous tense is to express the future.
3. The future tense is formed with *will* or *shall* + infinitive.
4. The past perfect tense is used to express the distant past.
5. Past and present tenses should not be used in the same sentence.

B. Comment on the meanings of the verbs in these utterances:
1. He's always dropping cigarette ash on the carpet.
2. Kevin Keegan scores for England at Hampden Park yesterday.
3. Borg serves to Connors.
4. It leaves at 6.30.
5. We'll wait until they arrive.
6. Pure water boils at 100° C.
7. I never saw Caruso sing.
8. I've never been to a Bob Dylan concert.
9. Hemingway wrote *The Old Man and the Sea*.
10. Dickens wrote novels.
11. Graham Greene wrote *The Power and the Glory*.
12. Joseph Heller has written three novels.
13. Gladstone would often take a hot water bottle filled with tea to bed.
14. I used to play football.

C. Comment on these errors.
1.x John uses to get up early.
2.x My brother lives in Kent for six years.
3.x Did you finish your homework yet?
4.x We've been in London yesterday.
5.x Dinosaurs had died out millions of years ago.

D. Comment on the effectiveness of this practice exercise:
PUT THE VERBS IN THE FOLLOWING SENTENCES INTO THE CORRECT TENSES:

1. He (go) to bed late last night.
2. Willy (never be) to Paris.
3. John (drink) heavily but now he's a teetotaller.
4. The Blues (be born) in the Mississippi Delta.
5. Buddy Holly (give) a concert just before he died.
6. West Germany (win) the 1974 World Cup.

E. Some uses of the simple present tense are exemplified in **B.** above.

Here is a more exhaustive list of uses.

(a) Pair the uses in the L.H. column with the examples in the R.H. column, and (b) place them in order to indicate teaching priorities.

1. Expresses habits.	Willy gets up at 7 every day.
2. Expresses action happening at time of statement.	Sugar dissolves in warm water.
3. Expresses general truths.	The Carlisle bus arrives at noon.
4. Expresses predictable, regularly occurring events in the future.	Joes smokes heavily. Mary speaks fluent Spanish.
5. Expresses routine.	Carter calls for energy summit.
6. Used in newspaper headlines to express recent past events.	Keegan passes to Hughes.
7. Expresses facts about the present.	We'll phone you as soon as we get home.
8. Expresses the future after certain time expressions.	

SECTION NINETEEN

A. State whether the word in **heavy** type in these utterances are verbs, adjectives or nouns.
1. **Seeing** is **believing**.
2. He's **waiting** for a taxi.

3. He's **playing** a **waiting** game.
4. Few people like **going** to the dentist's.
5. 'I hope you don't mind my **asking** . . .'
6. He watched her **crossing** the room.
7. They've just done a **listening** exercise.
8. The school is **being** redecorated.
9. **Being** a doctor, he was able to help.
10. She went upstairs **cursing** and **grumbling**.

B. Replace the words in **heavy** type in these utterances by a different word (not ending in -ing) which would fit in grammatically; the meaning is irrelevant.
   e.g. Willy hates **dancing**
     –Willy hates cabbage.
   1. The kettle is **boiling**.
   2. The film was **exciting**.
   3. 'I'm looking forward to **going to London**.'
   4. 'We had pork, roast potatoes and **sprouting** broccoli for lunch yesterday.'
   5. 'I'm not accustomed to **eating out**.'
   6. 'Stop **talking**.'

C. Comment on the differences between the utterances in each of the following pairs:
   1. He stopped to look at the newspaper.
      He stopped looking at the newspaper.
   2. 'Did you remember to lock the back door?'
      'Do you remember locking the back door?'
   3. 'Do you like dancing?'
      'Do you like to dance?'
   4. 'Do you like dancing?'
      'Would you like to dance?'
   5. She saw the burglar climb through the window.
      She saw the burglar climbing through the window.
   6. I regret telling you that your road tax is overdue.
      I regret to tell you that your road tax is overdue.

D. Comment on the errors in these utterances; put them right.
   1.x He has great difficulty to speak English.

2.x I enjoyed to visit Cambridge yesterday.

3.x He's used to go to bed late.

4.x I'm looking forward to hear from you.

5.x He tried starting his car but the battery was flat.

6.x I've always been interested to take photographs of old buildings.

7.x I don't feel like to go for a walk now.

8.x I'm very pleased seeing you.

SECTION TWENTY

A. Ask questions to elicit these answers (focusing on the word(s) in **heavy** type in each case).
1. 'It's **green**.'
2. 'A **green** one.'
3. 'The **green** one.'
4. '**Dangerously**.'
5. '**Quite frequently** – about once a week, in fact.'
6. '**Badly**.'
7. 'Oh, he's a **good** dancer.'
8. '**Nearby**.'

B. Account for the errors in these utterances.
1.x Sally works hardly.
2.x My friend speaks very well English.
3.x How is the weather today?
4.x Aberdeen is very far from London.
5.x I've just been to visit my ill friend.
6.x That's not a very usually colour for a car.
7.x My sister is elder than I am.
8.x He spoke to her friendlily.

C. Why do you think foreign learners may have problems with the words in **heavy** type in these utterances?
1. The baby is rather **poorly** today.
2. We have been visiting a **stately** home.
3. You should work **hard** and play **hard**.
4. Hold **tight**!

39

5. My brother isn't very **well**.
6. He has an **elderly** uncle in Cardiff.

D. Which of these utterances might be made
   (*a*) by an Eskimo in Zambia
   (*b*) by an Eskimo in Britain
   (*c*) by a Zambian in Britain
   (*d*) by a Zambian in Greenland
   1. 'It's too hot here.'
   2. 'It's rather cold here.'
   3. 'It's too cold here.'
   4. 'It's quite warm here.'
   What are the factors influencing the choice of *quite*, *rather* and *too* to modify adjectives and adverbs?

SECTION TWENTY-ONE

A. Some of the following sentences are correct and some are not. Sort out the incorrect ones and put them right.
   1. Peru, which is a very poor country, is known as the homeland of the Incas.
   2. The book, that you lent me last week, is on the shelf over there.
   3. He who laughs last laughs longest.
   4. Can you tell me more about the man you saw last night?
   5. Last week we went to see *Superman* which is a very good film but we couldn't stay till the end.
   6. Alexander Fleming, whose wife still lives in Athens, died some years ago.
   7. Alexander Fleming was the doctor who discovered penicillin.
   8. *The Times*, that is known internationally as the voice of Britain, was not printed for several months during 1979.
   9. *Kojak* was an American T.V. series, which was very popular in Britain.
   10. *Kojak*, which was very popular in Britain, was an American T.V. series.

11. When I was down in town I bumped into my cousin who told me the news.
12. The man that did most for race relations in the United States was Martin Luther King.

Why has the comma become such an important feature in these sentences?

B. What is the function of a defining (restrictive) relative clause? What is the function of a non-defining (non-restrictive) relative clause?

Would you say non-defining relative clauses are

(a) common

(b) quite common

or (c) fairly uncommon in spoken English? Why?

C. Why do you think some foreign learners find it difficult to understand (and produce, when appropriate) sentences like these?

1. The story you've just told me sounds plausible.
2. 'I've told you before to be careful of people offering something for nothing.'
3. 'Everywhere you go you hear the same complaint.'
4. He failed his exam again, which naturally disappointed him.
5. 'Nothing I have heard about him changes my opinion of him.'
6. An ammeter is an instrument used for measuring the strength of an electric current.

D. Comment on these utterances in the light of Ex. **A** and **C** above.

1. The girl in the red dress is beautiful.
2. They have just bought the old cottage on the hill above the village.
3. Please put out your cigarettes in the ashtray by the door.

E. Account for these foreign learner errors:

1.x The teacher lives opposite is a friend of mine.

2.x The student which you spoke to yesterday is absent today.

3.x The student who you spoke to him yesterday is absent today.

4.x *'Superman?* That's the film I got bored during.'

5.x 'She's not the little girl whom I once knew.'

6.x *'Superman,* that I saw last week, is a boring film.'

F. Comment on these sentences:
1. It was Clara that you saw waiting at the corner.
2. It could have been Fred that rang you last night.
3. It was last Friday that I first felt ill.
4. Where was it that you spent the weekend?
5. 'What we want is Watney's!' (slogan).
6. 'What you really believe is what is important.'

SECTION TWENTY-TWO

A. What do all these utterances have in common?
1. 'What do you want to drink?'
2. 'Can you help me?'
3. 'Only by using a powerful microscope can you see the intricate cell-structure.'
4. Hardly had he arrived when the 'phone rang.
5. 'You really should pay him back, shouldn't you?'
6. 'Pop' goes the weasel.
7. 'Here comes Willy at last!'
8. '. . . and so say all of us!'
9. 'Under no circumstances must you contact the police.'
10. So be it.
11. 'Willy hasn't finished yet and neither have I.'
12. 'Preparing to throw now is the world recorder-holder Al Feuerbach.'
13. 'Were you to ask me again, I might accept.'

B. Account for the inversion of subject and verb in each of the examples above.

C. Explain the difference between these two types of inversion.

Type 1 { Nor do I.
Seldom do you hear such a delightful rendering of that aria.
On no condition does he lend his car.

Type 2 { There goes Charlie.
'Hey-ho!' says Rowley.
Down the hill rolls the ball.

D. Explain the apparent inconsistency between the sentences in each pair.

a) Here comes my friend. *vs.* Here she comes.

b) Up into the clear blue sky soared the bird. *vs.* Up into the clear blue sky it soared.

E. Explain what is wrong with these utterances. Produce at least one acceptable version of each one.

1.x They go often to London.

2.x My sister plays marvellously tennis.

3.x 'I'm giving my daughter a cuddly pink new teddy for Christmas.'

4.x 'Where's your car?' 'I've lent John and his friends it.'

5.x 'Always I make that mistake!'

6.x 'That's a man's old coat.' (But note the ambiguity in your corrected version!)

7.x 'Nowhere am I going this evening. I'm staying at home.'

Unit Three

SECTION ONE

A. Look carefully at the following sentences.
  1. Pick that book up, will you ?
  2. How's Bill?
     He's picking up.
  3. He's been picked to play for England.
  4. Why are you always picking quarrels?
  5. He's the pick of a bad bunch.
  6. I picked up a hitch hiker at Stumps Cross.
  7. I'll pick you up at six.
  8. He's always picking his nose.
  9. I need to buy a new pick before we go climbing again.
  10. He's a pickpocket.
  11. Don't pick people to pieces all the time.
  12. He got in by picking the lock.

Questions
  1) If you were teaching vocabulary to an intermediate group and you were advised by your syllabus or text book to teach the word *pick*, what teaching decisions would you make?
  2) A class were doing a comprehension exercise in which the sentence, *I'll pick you up at ten* occurred. A student asked, 'What does *pick* mean?' and was told by the teacher to look it up in a dictionary. Comment on the teacher's answer.
  3) What answer would you have given to the student's question in 2 above?
  4) What is wrong with the following method of teaching the word *port*?
     Teacher: I noticed most of you got wrong the question about the ship not being able to get into port. Copy down the following definitions of *port*, learn them for homework and then write five sentences of your own using *port*.

44

pcrt = a harbour; a gate or gateway; carriage, bearing; to carry a weapon diagonally across and close to the body; left-hand side of a ship; strong sweet, dark red wine of Portugal.

B. 1) Look carefully at the following pairs of sentences and then say in what ways the words in **heavy** type are similar and in what ways they are different.
  1. *a)* Did you know that Ali has become a **rebel**?
     b) He hasn't. He's become a **freedom fighter**.
  2. *a)* I fancy Alice. She's really **slim**.
     b) No, she's **skinny**.
  3. *a)* He really is **mean**.
     b) I wouldn't say that, I would say he was **thrifty**.
  4. *a)* He's **very fat**, isn't he?
     b) He is. In fact I'd go as far as to say he's **obese**.
  5. *a)* He wears rather **feminine** clothes.
     b) **Effeminate** would be more accurate.

  2) What important vocabulary teaching points do the above pairs of sentences suggest to you?

C. 1) Replace the words in **heavy** type in the following sentences with one of the words from the following list: *shoes, pen, meat, seat, picture.*
  1. Look at this **drawing**.
  2. I bought a new pair of **boots**.
  3. Lend me that **biro**, will you?
  4. I think we'll have **steak** for dinner.
  5. Put it on the **chair**, will you?
  6. That's a nice **photo**.
  7. That **sofa** is not very comfortable.
  8. I like your new **moccasins**.
  9. Is this your **fountain pen**?
  10. I'll have that **lamb** please.
  11. Did you do that **painting**?
  12. Sit in that **armchair** there.
  13. That blue **ballpoint** is mine.
  14. Let's sit down on this **bench**.

  2) What does the above exercise suggest to you about the

45

teaching of vocabulary to beginners and to advanced students?

D. 1) What do you think might have caused the errors in the following sentences?
    1.x I fractured a cup when I was washing up.
    2.x He ejected the dog from the kitchen.
    3.x Don't feign to me.
    4.x Be careful. That bridge is feeble.
    5.x Your ball pierced my window.
    6.x I desire an ice-cream.
    7.x Don't worry. I'll manufacture another paper-aeroplane for your Willy.
    8.x The buses were on strike so we had to march all the way to town.

    2) What conclusions about the teaching of vocabulary does a consideration of the above errors lead you to?

E. 1) What is missing from the following definitions?
    mate = *friend*
    fag = *cigarette*
    bird = *girl*
    boss = *master or manager*
    guy = *man*

    2) What errors could the learning of such definitions lead to? Give one example for each word.

    3) What important points about the teaching of vocabulary does this exercise suggest to you?

F. Look at the diagrams on page 47.
What ideas do they suggest to you for the teaching of vocabulary?

G. Look at the examples of the use and misuse of the words in each of the following pairs of English words. Then come to conclusions about:
1) the difference between the words in each pair;
2) the criteria for deciding whether two words are interchangeable;

46

Diagrams for Exercise F

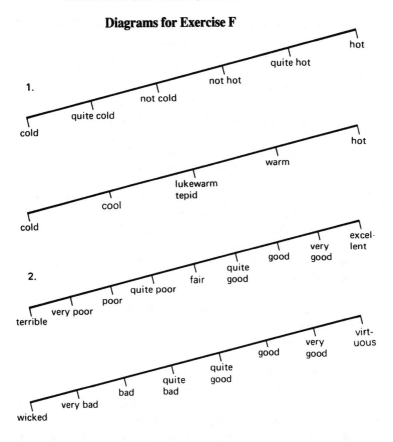

3) the use of synonyms (or near synonyms) in the teaching of vocabulary.
a) *reach/arrive*
    1. We reached home at ten.
    2. We arrived home at ten.
    3. I reached the French border at six.
    4.x I arrived the French border at six.
    5. I reached that conclusion last night.
    6. I arrived at that conclusion last night.
    7. He has just arrived.
    8.x He has just reached.
    9.x He arrived out his hand.

47

10. He reached out his hand.
11.x We reached back at ten.
12. We arrived back at ten.
13. Can I reach you at the office?
14.x Can I arrive you at the office?

b) *brave/courageous*
    1. That was a brave decision.
    2. That was a courageous decision.
    3. He's a brave man.
    4. He's a courageous man.
    5. He braved the storm.
    6.x He couraged the storm.
    7. Making the decision to resign took great courage.
    8.x Making the decision to resign took great bravery.
    9. Rescuing that boy from the fire was an act of great bravery.
    10. Rescuing that boy from the fire was an act of great courage.
    11. He didn't have the courage of his convictions.
    12.x He didn't have the bravery of his convictions.
    13. Don't lose courage.
    14.x Don't lose bravery.
    15. Hard luck, that was a brave try.
    16. Hard luck, that was a courageous try.

c) *put up/accommodate*
    1. Can you accommodate a party of ten students?
    2. Can you put up a party of ten students?
    3. Hey, Bill, can you put me up tonight?
    4.x Hey, Bill, can you accommodate me tonight?

H. 1) Look at the following sentences and then make conclusions about the use of opposites in the teaching of vocabulary.

a) *light/dark*
    1. It was a light evening.
    2. It was a light load.
    3. It was a dark day for England.

b) *old/new*
    1. He's an old man.

    2. He's an old friend.

    3. I'll do it for old times' sake.

    4. He's like a new man.

    5. I think we'll try a new way to work today.

c) *rich/poor*

    1. Poor man, he's hurt.

    2. That cake is too rich.

    3. That's a poor idea.

    4. He's rich in ideas.

d) *tall/short*

    1. That's a tall building.

    2. That's a tall order.

    3. I always seem to be short of breath.

    4. I'm too short to join the police force.

    5. This rope is too short.

e) *rough/smooth*

    1. He's very rough.

    2. He got a rough deal.

    3. It was a rough match.

    4. This material is smooth.

    5. He's a very smooth person.

f) *work/leisure*

    1. He works in a leisurely way.

    2. Mozart's works will live for ever.

    3. He's at the works.

    4. We need to educate people for leisure as well as work.

2) For each of the above pairs decide whether you would ever teach them together and give the reasons for your decisions.

I. 1) The following were sentences used by different teachers to help them to exemplify the meaning of *amazed*. Look carefully at each example and then say why you think it is a good or a bad teaching example.

    1. I was amazed when he told me.

    2. I've never been so amazed in my life.

    3. He was absolutely amazed when he found out.

    4. I was really amazed when he told me he had failed

the exam. The reason I was so surprised was that he had been getting very high marks all term. I was even more amazed when I found out that I had passed as all term I had been getting low marks.

   5. I was amazed by his death. I had never expected him to die so soon.

2) As a result of doing the above exercise what conclusions have you come to about examples used to help teach the meanings of new words?

3) Write teaching examples for the following:
   careful; clumsy;
   slippery; decide.

J. In a comprehension test you have asked your students to write a sentence of their own using *swept* as it is used in the passage (i.e. *Mary swept the carpet every morning*).
Look at the sentences you got from your students. What do they tell you?

A. She swept the carpets twice a week.

B. Jane swept the carpet a lot.

C. Have you swept the carpet yet?

D. He swept it. I saw him.

E. Mary swept the carpet before she went to work.

F. They didn't sweep the carpet very often.

K. For each of the following deduce the meaning of the underlined nonsense word(s) and say what clues you found in the text to help you make the deduction.

   1. 'I found this <u>nibbit</u> in your pocket when I took your coat to be <u>slinned</u>.'
   'Oh yes, I put it in my pocket in case I was hungry at the football match.'
   'I prefer the ones with chocolate on myself.'
   'So do I. That's probably why I didn't eat it. When will my coat be ready?'
   'Tomorrow morning.'
   'I hope they get all the marks and stains out this time. I want to look smart at my interview.'

   2. 'Did you have to <u>ding</u> him so hard?'

'He was very naughty.'

'But you really hurt him.'

'I know, I hurt my hand too. It was only his leg though.'

'He'll soon get over it.'

3. I was sitting in the garden reading when I felt a drop of rain. I didn't want the <u>glogget</u> to get wet so I got up, folded it up and went to put it in the garage with the other garden seats. When I saw the garage I was furious. It was so <u>unseddy</u>. I'd told the kids to put all their toys in the trunk to keep the garage <u>seddy</u> but now there were toys all over the garage floor.

What vocabulary teaching points does the above exercise suggest to you?

L. 1) If the following words existed what do you think they would mean?

1. *reget*
2. *cardback*
3. *excessage*
4. *sublunar*
5. *bidaily*
6. *punkly*
7. *postthink*
8. *impossibliate*
9. *disrecommend*
10. *attendive*

2) What parts of speech (e.g. noun) would they be?

3) What vocabulary teaching points does this exercise suggest to you?

M. 1) Which sentences produced by the following substitution table are not acceptable or not normal in English?

1	2	3
It was	marvellous sensational amazing superlative superb incredible brilliant wonderful	to eat to watch to hear to drive

2) Can you make any valid generalisations as a result of doing the above exercise?

3) What conclusions does the above exercise lead you to regarding the teaching of the words in column 2?

N. 1) Try to make as many acceptable sentences as possible from the following substitution table.

2) Make statements about the differences in meaning between the words in column 2.

1	2	3	4
I've	bought purchased hired rented rented out sold borrowed leased acquired lent let loaned	a the my	house car money business pen tent maid television picture dog

0. Comment on the following vocabulary exercise.

Decide whether the words in column *A* can be used together with each of the numbered words. If two words can be used together put a tick in the relevant box. If two words cannot be used together put a cross.

A	*1* believer	*2* supporter	*3* customer	*4* gardener	*5* student	*6* reader	*7* vegetarian
keen		✓					
fervent							
enthusiastic							
fanatical							
interested							
zealous							

SECTION TWO

A. Look at the verbs in these utterances, and group them into two separate categories according to whether they are followed by adverbs or prepositions.

1. **Drink up** quickly.
2. He **switched** the light **off**.
3. 'Is this story true or did you **make** it **up**?'
4. He has just **applied for** a new job.
5. We **called on** Willy yesterday.
6. In Germany, young men are **called up** at the age of 18.
7. Water **consists of** hydrogen and oxygen.
8. He was **looked upon** as a hero.

B. Comment on the verbs in these utterances.

1. 'You'll have to **catch up on** what you've missed.'
2. 'You mustn't **put up with** that!'
3. Most western countries have **done away with** capital punishment.
4. 'You must **drop in on** us some time.'

53

C. Turn these utterances into the passive and comment on the stress patterns in each.
1. Someone will have to speak to him firmly.
2. Someone will have to put this work aside.
3. Nobody can account for three of the crew.
4. They cleaned the house up after the party.
5. Someone has filled this form in.
6. Someone has laid up a lot of ships in the south west of England.
7. Someone has shut down the steelworks.
8. Someone has worn this record out.

D. Comment on the *meanings* of the verbs in **heavy** type.
1. Some learners **catch on** very quickly.
2. 'You're always **answering back**!'
3. 'This milk has **gone off**!'
4. 'Your new dress needs **to be let down**.'
5. Our sponsors have **let** us **down**.
6. 'We'll have to **lay in** extra sugar supplies.'
7. 'You shouldn't keep on **running** your friends **down**.'
8. He was **put out** by your attitude.
9. '**Stand up**!'
10. He **ran away** from home when he was 6.
11. 'What time did you **knock off** last night?'
12. 'My French needs **brushing up**.'

E. Comment on the effectiveness of this exercise:
REPLACE THE VERBS UNDERLINED IN THESE EXAMPLES WITH PHRASAL OR PREPOSITIONAL VERBS
1. He had three teeth extracted yesterday.
2. He was raised in Scotland.
3. She resembles her mother.
4. The match has been postponed till next week.
5. You're always disparaging your brother.
6. That paragraph can be omitted.
7. His accent betrayed him as a Welshman.
8. Everyone feels the need to escape for a while.
9. Dinosaurs became extinct millions of years ago.
10. 'We must reduce our outgoings.'

Unit Four

SECTION ONE

A. Look carefully at the following sentences and think about the function of the words in **heavy** type.

1. Have you given **it** to **him** yet?
2. Are we seeing **them** again tonight?
3. Did you buy **it** from **him**?
4. Have **they** seen **it** before?
5. If I see **him** with **her** again I'll tell you.
6. Why did **she** get angry?
   He was very drunk.
7. **Hers** is beautiful.

Questions

1. Why is it not clear what the above sentences refer to?
2. What is required to make the reference of the above sentences clear?
3. Re-write the sentences to make their reference clear.
4. When would your sentences be more appropriate than the sentences above?
5. When would the above sentences be more appropriate than your sentences?
6. Are there any situations in which some of your sentences would actually be considered incorrect?
7. 'he', 'she', 'it', 'they', 'him', 'her', and 'them' are personal pronouns. What do you think the main function of these pronouns is?
8. 'I', 'we' and 'you' are also personal pronouns. Why cannot you replace them with nouns in the above sentences?
   How are they different in function from the other personal pronouns?
9. 'hers' is similar in function to 'her'. What is the difference?

B. 1) What has caused the breakdown in communication in the following conversations?

55

1. *A* Are they going there again?
     B Where?
2. *A* I saw him then.
     B When?
3. *A* I'm doing those then.
     B Which?
4. *A* Did you buy that there?
     B What?

2) What generalisations can you make about the functions of 'that', 'those', 'there' and 'then'?

3) What word in each of the conversations could have caused a breakdown in communication but did not? Say why you think these words did not result in lack of communication.

C. 1) Why is there very little danger of a breakdown in communication in the following sentences?

1. I'll give you this instead.
2. Are these yours?
3. I'll see you here at six.
4. Let's eat here now.

2) What do you think the main difference in function is between:

1. *this*, *those*, *here* and *now*
    and
2. *that*, *those*, *there* and *then*

D. Look carefully at the following utterances.

1. *A* 'He broke her favourite vase.'
     B 'That was very valuable.'
     A 'That was very careless.'
2. *A* 'Don't worry. There'll be nobody in the house, we'll be on the road with the picture in ten minutes' time.'
     B 'I still don't like the idea.'
     A 'This is it now. Stop the car.'
     B 'This is crazy.'

What is the main difference in function between the two instances of *that* in 1 and between the two instances of *this* in 2?

E. 1. What is the potential difference in meaning between *a)* and *b)*?
   a) They were a different two books.
   b) They were two different books.
   What is the difference between the grammatical function of *different* in *a)* and *different* in *b)*?

   2. Rewrite the following sentence in two different ways to demonstrate its two possible meanings.
   I need some other clothes.
   What does the word *other* warn you to do in order to understand the sentence?

   3. *a)* What makes the following sentence ambiguous?
   We'll have to do more.
   b) Describe two situations in which the sentence would not be ambiguous. The sentence should not have the same meaning in both situations.

F. 1) What do the words in **heavy** type in the following sentences have in common?
   1. Your cooker is not working properly.
   I know, I need a new **one**.
   2. Does anyone want to go to the pub?
   Yes, I **do**.
   3. Has the London train gone?
   I think **so**.
   4. My mother fusses and nags me all the time.
   Mine **does** too.
   5. I'll have a pint of bitter.
   I'll have the **same**.
   6. Will the game be postponed?
   I hope **not**.
   7. Don't bother washing the cups.
   We can use the old **ones**.
   8. I didn't get a paper today. Can I borrow **yours**?
   9. Can you give me a lift in your car? **Mine** has broken down.

   2. The words in **heavy** type have very similar grammatical functions. However they can be divided into four distinct groups. The words in 1, 5 and 7 belong in group one;

those in 2 and 4 in group two; those in 3 and 6 in group three; and those in 8 and 9 in group four.
What is the difference between the four groups?

G. 1. What do the following utterances in **heavy** type have in common?
1. Mark bought a plant **and Lynn a basket of flowers.**
2. Would you like to hear another song? **I know a lot.**
3. What did you think of the lectures?
   Two were quite good but two were awful.
4. I thought that one of the twins would get into the team **but I was surprised when both were selected.**
5. Has he gone?
   Yes, he has.
6. Janet should have been informed **but I don't think she has been.**
7. **Bill scored two and Fred one.**
8. Has she been laughing?
   No, crying.
9. What should I have done?
   Phoned the police.

2. The above underlined utterances could be divided into two groups.
Allocate each utterance to a group and describe the difference between Group One and Group Two.

3. Try to work out generalisations from the above examples.

H. Look carefully at the following sentences.
A. 1. I like football **and** I like rugby.
2. I like rugby **and** I like football.
3. **As well as** football I like rugby.
4. I like rugby **as well as** football.
5. **In addition to** football I like rugby.
6. I like rugby **in addition to** football.
7. I like football. **Also** I like rugby.
8. I like rugby. **Also** I like football.
9. I like football. **In addition** I like rugby.
10. I like rugby. **In addition** I like football.

58

B.   1.   It is an old car **but** it never lets me down.

      2.   It is an old car. **However** it never lets me down.

      3.   **Although** it is an old car it never lets me down.

      4.   It never lets me down **but** it is an old car.

      5.   It never lets me down. **However** it is an old car.

      6.   It never lets me down **although** it is an old car.

1.   Are there any potential differences in meaning between the different sentences in *A*? If so say what they are.

2.   The words underlined in *A* are examples of words and phrases which can be used to link two statements, ideas etc. together. They represent three different types of such words and phrases. *As well as*, *and* and *also* belong to different types. Distinguish between the three types and allocate each of the underlined words to one of your types.

3.   What are the differences in meaning between the sentences in *B*?

4.   Allocate each of the underlined words in *B* to one of the types you have established in 2 above.

I.

instead	in that case
and also	similarly
in fact	consequently
despite this	then
however	so
on the other hand	for example
meanwhile	therefore
at the same time	on the contrary
as a matter of fact	on account of this
likewise	finally
in any case	furthermore
because of this	thus
previously	with this in mind
for instance	as well as
for this purpose	besides

1.   Make up sentences exemplifying the use of each of the items in the above list.

2. Place each item in one of the types established in H above.
3. Place each item in the appropriate column below.

Exemplification	Sequence first	Reason for this reason	Result as a result	Purpose	Comparison in the same way
Addition	Contrast nevertheless even so	Correction rather at least	Dismissal anyhow	Reinforce-ment moreover	Time

4. When you have filled in the columns examine the expressions in each column and then comment on the differences in use between the expressions.

J. Identify, correct and explain the errors in the following sentences.
1. The ship finally sank this morning. Meanwhile in Canada there has been an unprecedented heatwave.
2. It was a tremendously exciting match. Nevertheless I hope you enjoyed it.
3. I don't like musicals. Anyhow I'll come with you.
4. I don't like jazz. On the contrary I like folk music.
5. It was really cold in the factory. In that case they refused to work.

K. 1. Complete the following sentences.
   1. We all kept quiet. That seemed the best _____ .
   2. Any ideas where I should stay in Hong Kong? I've never been to the _____ before.

3. What shall I do with all this equipment?
   Leave the st_____ here. We'll come back for it later.
4. I thought we were going to London today. I don't
   know where you got that _____ from.
5. Where shall I put this hairdryer?
   Put the t_____ away in that cupboard.
6. Bill's been stealing apples again. I'll have to teach
   that _____ a lesson.
7. Mrs Biggins has been spreading rumours about you
   again. That _____ is a damn nuisance.
8. She's feeding her dog. That cr_____ eats more food
   than I do.

2. Make generalisations about the words you have used to
   fill in the blanks above.

L. What are the teaching implications of the discoveries you
have made as a result of doing the exercises in this Unit?

Unit Five

SECTION ONE

A. Look carefully at the following dialogues.
1.   *A* – Would you like a cigarette?
     B – No thanks.
     A – It's O.K. I've got plenty more.
     B – I don't smoke.
2.   *A* – It's raining, isn't it?
     B– Yes, it is.
     A – I'd better go and get my mac then.
     B – Could you get mine as well please?
3.   *A* – It's two o'clock.
     B – Don't worry. I'm nearly ready.
     A – It'll take us at least fifteen minutes to get there.
     B – Do you ever stop worrying?

Analyse each of the utterances in the above dialogues in the same way as the following example.

		Type	*Purpose*
1.	*A*	Interrogative	Offer

B. 1.   Describe situations in which the following exchanges would make sense.
    1)   *A* – The grass needs cutting.
        B – It's nearly ten o'clock.
        A – He'll wait.
        B – Like last week and the week before.
        A – The Robinsons are coming tomorrow.
        B – It's starting to rain now anyway.
    2)   *A* – Shall we stop for a while?
        B – If you want.
        A – The Cow's quite good, isn't it?
        B – If you say so.
        A– We met your friend Jane last time, didn't we?
        B – My mother will be worried.
    3)   *A* – Hallo.
        B – Bob?

A – I'm not coming tonight.

B – He's already gone.

A – Already?

B – Try Ted's.

2. Analyse each utterance in each of the above dialogues in the same way as the following example.

	Type	Purpose
1. A	Declarative	Getting somebody to do something

3. What implications for teaching do you think your analysis of the exchanges in 1 and 2 reveals?

C. The imperative sentence, *Do it now* can be interpreted in different ways according to the situation in which it was uttered. It could be interpreted as any one of the following:

1. *command*
2. *advice*
3. *appeal*
4. *instruction*
5. *warning*

1. List the set of conditions which you think must prevail for the sentence to be interpreted as each of the five speech acts listed above.

   e.g. *1. command*

   a) A in authority over B

   b) B accepts authority of A

   c) A wants B to do something

2. How can such a listing of conditions help the teacher?

D. Read the following paragraph.

The suggestion that all industries should be nationalised is ridiculous. Can you imagine the cost and the chaos? Look what happened to the railways. And the steel industry. No. Instead let us encourage private enterprise. Only then will we have initiative and thus prosperity.

NOW ANSWER THE FOLLOWING QUESTIONS

1. What speech act (see Q4) does the question, *Can you imagine . . .* perform?
2. What speech act is performed by, *Look what happened to the railways?*
3. What two propositions does *instead* connect?
4. What does *then* refer to in the last sentence?
5. What is the function of *thus* in the last sentence?
6. The following analysis of the strategic structure of the above paragraph is wrong. Correct it.
   a) Statement.
   b) Question.
   c) Exemplification.
   d) Refutation.
   e) Conclusion.
   f) Qualification of conclusion.

E. Read the following.

We have a problem. Yesterday I was told that we couldn't have any more books this year as our budget has been spent. That means of course no tapes for the winter term. However I think I've got an answer. If your brother can lend us the tapes from his school we can lend him that spare set of "Mullens" for the term.

NOW ANSWER THE FOLLOWING QUESTIONS

1. What is the problem? How do you know?
2. What does *that* refer to in sentence 3?
3. What two propositions does *however* (in sentence 4) connect?
4. Does the *we* include or exclude the addressee? How do you know?
5. What does *Mullens* refer to? How do you know?
6. What implications for teaching have you discovered from doing 1–5 above?

F. Identify and analyse the errors in the following extract from a student's work.

The most significant influence is the purchasing power of

consumers. Nowadays, people tend to use central heaters rather than coal. Furthermore, the level of income altered the life style of the consumers. They prefer to use modern electrical appliances such as the electric kettle.

Another factor is the change in transportation. The increase in petrol led to the increase in transport especially the electrification of railway and motor vehicles. However, other types of industries increased from 15,210 million therms to 18,455 million therms as a result of the decrease in the iron and steel industry.

Unit Six

SECTION ONE

A. *1.* Correct the errors in the following sentences and say what you think might have caused each of the errors.

   1.x My father is a **fisher**.

   2.x I **am seeing** a lion in that cage.

   3.x He **like** football.

   4.x He **leaves** in a large house.

   5.x When I **will go** there tomorrow I will visit Mary.

   6.x She's beautiful, **isn't it**?

   7.x He **has gone** there this morning.

   8.x Will you **borrow** me your car?

   9.x He **has robbed** all my money.

  10.x I rang up **so I booked** the tickets.

  11.x He **had gone** to London yesterday at two.

  12.x He **was wounded** in the car crash.

  13.x If **he asked** I would have helped him.

  14.x Suddenly **there came a friend** to me.

  15.x We were **to** noisy.

  16.x **This couldn't car us a** rap.

  17.x I'm going to the lake **for swimming**.

  18.x **My mother she is** very old.

  19.x Mary doesn't like Jim. **He** says he is selfish.

  20.x I have stopped **to play** football because of my injury.

  2. Make generalisations about potential causes of learner errors from an analysis of the errors above.

B. Look at the following transcript of part of a conversation between two elementary learners and then:

  1. List all the errors.

  2. Correct the errors.

  3. Select types of errors and say what you think might have caused the students to make the errors.

  4. Say which of the errors you would correct if you were the teacher listening to the conversation. Give reasons for your selection.

A. I will be football player when I will be back to my home.

B. I will be professor in school.

A. What for?

B. I will enjoy. It will be nice to be teach.

A. No, it is bore. Football will be interest. It will be rich.

B. Professor will be rich too.

A. No, not true. Football player will be very much rich.

B. In my country football player not be rich, not give the money.

A. In my country he will be give lot of money.

C. Compare the following extracts from an elementary learner's work book. The second extract was written two weeks after the first.

1. *Yesterday I bought book from shop. It cost £2. I read last night . . .*

2. *Last week I buyed a new shirt from a shop in Cambridge. It cost me £10. I weared it at the party . . .*

1. What are the main differences between the two extracts?

2. What do you think might have been responsible for the differences?

D. What can you discover about the learner's problems from reading the following extract from his work?

My brother lives in a village but work in a town. Usually he cycles to his work however sometimes he goes by bus. His work is very tiring nevertheless he plays football and train when he comes home.

E. 1. List and correct all the errors in the following extract from a learner's composition. Underline all those errors which you think should be given remedial attention by the teacher.

A TERRIBLE DREAM

One day in September, the weather was fine and I worked the whole day. I was very tired, I went to bed and fell asleep. Suddenly there came a friend to me and asked me to go with him. That friend died 5 years before, so it was very strange to meet him. I went with my friend. We walked in a very dark hall and when there were stairs, we went upstairs. We went to a room to see a garden of flowers. But there were no flowers, there was only a very strange man, his shin was very strange. He had a scarp in his face, he was very ugly. He beconed me to come near. I was afraid, but I had to go near because in my back there were two men holding a gun. I went near, the man had a knife in his hand.

He wanted to murder me because his friend died two weeks before from an accident with my father. I said I could manage it, so he got a lot of money. He would gave me three hours to do everything in order. My friend and I were tied on a chair. We made up a story.

When the man came back, we should run away as fast as we could to the nearest police station.

After a time they came back, they had talked to my father. He wouldn't give any money they said, so they had to kill me. He took his knife to my heart. He want to come near with his knife. I shouted very hard and my mother came to my room. She asked what there was happened. I said that it was only a bad dream.

2.   Make generalisations about the errors in the above extract.

F. The following is the transcript of a tape of an advanced learner telling the story of a cartoon.

1. List and correct all the errors.
2. Which of the errors do you think might impede communication?

'In a little local village Mr and Mrs Robinson wanted to watch the weekend film, when Mr Robinson switched on television he saw it didn't seem to work, so he went outside to discover that the television aerial had been broken down. That's why he tried to fix the ladder, to get a ladder and get on to the roof to fix it . . . The ladder fell away, so he had to shout for help. His wife came outside and saw what was happening so she immediately called the fire brigade. When they arrived they succeeded in getting Mr Robinson safely on earth again. The three of them, Mr and Mrs Robinson and

the man . . . were standing there. Then at home Mrs Robinson made a hot cup of tea, and they were sitting together there, trying to watch T.V. to see a part of the weekend film but when they switched on television, the only thing they saw was "The End".'

G. Read the following extract from a student's story and then:
 1. List and correct all the errors.
 He has been taken to hospital to see his friend. He came back an hour later but then went home. He said he had only been in hospital for ten minutes because the bus broke down and he must walk. He arrived at the hospital after closing time but because he has lonely the nurse granted him permission to see his friend shortly. If he told me he was going to the hospital I could give him a lift. Then he would have stayed with his friend a lot longer.
 2. Give an example from the extract of each of the following types of error:
  1. A lexical confusion which could impede communication.
  2. An expression which is too formal for the situation.
  3. An adverbial confusion which in another context could impede communication.
  4. A prepositional phrase confusion which in another context could impede communication.
  5. A tense error which could cause a time reference confusion.

COMMENTARIES

In this section possible answers to most of the questions are suggested. In some cases various other answers would be acceptable but are not included because of considerations of space.

A few of the questions are so open-ended and specific to the individual readers' own experience that it has been decided not to provide an answer.

Unit One

SECTION ONE

Commentary

A. 1. Below are some of the comments that could be made. Encouraging students to read only the classics of English literature does not necessarily help them to speak English well. Some of the reasons for this are as follows:

a) The classics were written a long time ago and therefore exemplify English expressions which are no longer current.

b) Many of the classics include dialogue which exemplifies regional dialects which are very different from the standard English dialect which we teach in the classroom (e.g. *b)* i)).

c) The syntax and style of the written English of the classics is very different from that of the spoken English of today (e.g. *b)* ii)).

d) There is no such thing as the *best English*. An utterance in English is good if it succeeds in communicating the speaker's or writer's meaning and intention and if it is appropriate to the situation in which it is used. Reading only the classics can give the learner the false impression that he should always try to use literary English.

e) It is important that learners of English are given

practice in reading the different types of modern written English which they are likely to be exposed to outside the classroom.

    f) Reading is a passive skill and merely practising it does not by itself help the learner to acquire the active skill of speaking in English.

2. The following are some of the points that could be made.

    a) A language cannot be said to be stupid because it is not completely regular and is not completely controlled by rules. No living language is completely regular and rule bound because living languages are organic and are constantly being changed by their users.

    b) It is common for learners of a language to think that their own language is logical and regular whereas the one they are learning is stupidly irregular. This is usually because they very seldom examine their own language whereas they are frequently called upon to examine the language they are learning. They also find their own language easy to use and assume that this is because it is logical and regular.

    c) English, like most other languages, is not rule bound. It has been influenced by many other languages (e.g. Anglo-Saxon, Latin, Greek, French) and it contains many apparent illogicalities. However, like all languages, it operates as a system of generalisations not as a system of absolute rules. Thus it is possible to make generalisations about the formation of the simple past tense in English (see *b*)3) but it is easy to think of exceptions to these generalisations. The important thing to remember is that when formulating generalisations about a language you should describe what people using the language actually do and not prescribe what they should do.

    d) No language follows rules. Languages evolve and then linguists attempt to describe them. In

71

describing them linguists sometimes unfortunately make it seem that the patterns and˙ regularities underlying the language are in fact rules to be obeyed by the users of the language.

e) There are some patterns in English that are extremely regular and could be taught as rules. The doubling of the consonant after short vowel sounds is one such *rule* (see *b*)1) as is the agreement in person between the statement and the tag in English question tags (see *b*)2).

3. The following are some of the points that could be made.

    1. In *b*(i), (ii) and (iii) the pupil has imitated the form of a structure used by the teacher. In each case the pupil has made an error because the form he has used has not been appropriate. In (i) he uses the present continuous tense but this is inappropriate when referring to an ailment or illness; in (ii) he uses the present perfect inappropriately to refer to a specific point of time in the past; and in (iii) he uses 'will' to refer to the future in a time clause in which the appropriate verb form is the simple present tense.

    2. It is obvious from the evidence in *b*) that learning a language purely through imitation of correct forms can lead to the making of errors even when the forms are imitated correctly. It is important to be able to reproduce the correct forms of English structures but it is also very important to know when to use them and when not to use them. This cannot be learned from the imitation of forms.

B. 1. In this statement the writer breaks all the rules that he imposes on his learners and thus demonstrates the frequent contradiction between actual usage and prescriptive rules. He uses *will* with *I*, he uses *who* instead of *whom* (*The pupils who I teach*), he splits an infinitive (*to always speak*) and he ends his sentence with the preposition *with*.

All the rules that he insists on (but breaks) refer to generalisations that used to be valid when describing the written English of the highly educated. None of them are valid today. They certainly do not describe what 'correct' speakers of English do today and therefore should not be imposed on learners of the language.

2. This statement illustrates the dangers of learning lists of uncommon words and then trying to ostentate the new words. The writer has learned the forms of many words that are not commonly used in English and has retained an approximate knowledge of their meaning. However he has not learned the restrictions on their use and his accumulation of inappropriate and unusual words will inevitably result in a ridiculous failure to communicate.

New words should be learned in context and not from lists and learners of English should be discouraged from trying to learn and use every *long* or unusual word they come across.

C. 1. English in its present form is not ancient at all and it is certainly not pure. It is the current stage in a process of evolution which has been influenced by contact with many other languages (e.g. Latin, Greek, French, Dutch) and with many regional varieties of English (e.g. Australian English, Indian English and American English). Change is inevitable in a language and borrowings and coinings are an important part of this change.

Such emotive words as *great*, *corruption*, *vulgar* and *pure* are not appropriate in a description of language development and it is pointless to *fight against* what has already happened to a language.

2. It is a common misconception that foreigners talk very quickly as what you do not understand appears to be said more quickly than what you do understand. The learner finds the teacher easier to understand than a stranger because he has got used to his accent and his speech mannerisms and because the teacher makes a deliberate attempt to make himself clearly understood.

It is important that learners are exposed to many

73

different voices and that they participate in authentic conversation as well as practice drills in the classroom. It is especially important that the teacher does not always talk to his learners in an artificially slow and precise way as what is gained in immediate convenience will not compensate for future frustration.

3. Grammar books and dictionaries are important sources of information about a language. They can teach someone about a language but they cannot teach anyone to use a language as they cannot expose the learner to language in real use and they do not provide any opportunities for practice or production.

4. There is no such thing as *incorrect English*. There are many regional varieties of English. Each one is different from the others but all are equally correct. Standard English is the variety of English normally taught to foreign learners as this is the variety used by all well-educated users of English regardless of their regional origins. The accent (i.e. way of pronouncing) normally taught to foreign learners is *R.P.* (*Received Pronunciation*). This accent is the one taught because it was the first one analysed and described and because many of the early English teachers and material designers spoke an approximation of it. However the users of this accent (often called *B.B.C.* or *Oxford English*) are in the minority and can be defined as educated speakers of English whose accent is entirely uninfluenced by the accent of their region of origin.

As most learners of English will eventually be exposed to many different English accents it is a good thing if some of their teachers are not *R.P.* speakers.

5. Many learners think that they have learned a structure when they have written down rules about it and have made up a few sentences exemplifying it. They do not realise that it is necessary to use a structure over and over again before it can be considered to have been learned.

Knowing a structure is not the same thing as being able to use a structure. The ability to use a structure only comes as a result of frequent meaningful practice of its use. Many learners get frustrated by long, mechanical drills that are so easy that they always get them right. There is no challenge and as far as they are concerned nothing else to learn. It is thus important to provide practice which is varied, stimulating and meaningful and which not only gives the learner the opportunity to reinforce his learning of the form of the structure but also helps him to realise when and how to use the structure.

6. Such a teacher will inevitably produce learners who stand out as being out of touch with current usage, who get frustrated by the discrepancy between what they are taught and what English speakers actually do and who are inhibited by the constant demand for correctness.

    Such a teacher also fails to appreciate the difference between spoken and written English and the fact that what is considered to be correct depends on the situation in which the language is being used. He also makes the arrogant mistake that a lot of experience automatically equals a lot of wisdom.

7. Language learning requires some noise as no effective learning can take place without practice. If the groups have been purposefully set up by the teacher to facilitate language practice and the ensuing noise is in the appropriate language and related to a planned objective then the teacher deserves praise.

8. The writer is engaging in a futile piece of prescription. He is saying that the grammar book and the dictionary have more authority than the language user. What the writer says is unacceptable is in fact common usage.

    As teachers we should concern ourselves with what is said not what we think ought to be said.

9. This statement is demonstrably untrue (e.g. *Have you found some?*; *I'll deal with any questions at the end*). However at an early stage of language learning it might be a useful over-simplification to make to certain learners providing that the truth is subsequently revealed.

10. This is demonstrably untrue (e.g. *to pity*, *to fear* and *to*

expect are verbs but not doing words; *running* – as in *running is good for you* – is a doing word but functions as a noun not a verb).

At no stage of learning is this a useful over-simplification as it misleads the learner without helping him to use the language.

11. This statement is also neither true nor useful. So many subjects can be neither people nor things (e.g. *What he says makes sense*) and very often the subject does not do any action (e.g. *He is hoping to go to university*).

12. Tense is not the same as time reference. The past tenses are often used with past time reference but not always (e.g. *I was thinking of going to the match tomorrow; I wondered if you would allow us to miss the meeting; If he came it would be too late*).

13. This statement is confusing as it is obvious that you can count money. It would be more accurate to say that uncountable nouns cannot be preceded by a number (e.g. **x** *two rices*; **x** *four monies*). N.B. **x** = incorrect utterance.

14. Spoken English and written English are two different varieties of the same language. Proficient native speakers of English frequently do things in conversation which would be considered errors in writing (e.g. *It's too expensive to buy for just . . . It's too complicated too. Frequent breakdowns, panic, more expense*). In fact the speaker himself uses contractions (*It's; they're*) which would be considered incorrect in a formal piece of writing.

15. *Will* is used in such clauses with the function of expressing *willingness* (e.g. *Let me know when he will do it*). The statement is designed to prevent such errors as, **x** *I will phone you when he will arrive*, and can be a fairly useful over-simplification if it is made less absolute (e.g. *not often* instead of *never*).

16. A good English speaker uses the type of English most suited to the situation. In some informal conversations slang is very suitable (e.g. an argument between friends in a pub about a football match).

Unit Two

SECTION ONE

Commentary

A. (N.B. these are working definitions which will later need to be refined and made more precise.)

1. A noun is a word which names. Nouns can be concrete (e.g. *table, tree, horse, finger, car*), abstract (e.g. *simplicity, glee, lateness, health*) or proper (e.g. *England, John, Guinness, Liverpool*).

2. A pronoun substitutes for a noun, e.g. *he, she, you, we, I, they, it, her, him, us, them, me, his, their, our, my, its*.

3. A transitive verb is a verb which has a direct object, e.g. *eats* in this sentence:
    John eats toast in the evenings.
    (*toast* is the direct object)

4. An intransitive verb is a verb without a direct object, e.g. *eats* in this sentence:
    John always eats at seven o'clock.

5. An infinitive is a standard verb form (without a subject) and is the form usually found as a dictionary headword, e.g. *eat, drink, listen, doubt.* An infinitive form appears with or without *to*:
    I want *to come.*
    He can't *swim.*

6. (*i*)   (*a*) Churchill (*b*) smoked (*c*) cigars (direct object)

    (*ii*) (*a*) Few women (*b*) smoke (*c*) cigars (direct object)

    (*iii*) (*a*) Smoking (*b*) causes (*c*) health problems (direct object)

    (*iv*) (*a*) Cigarettes (*b*) are (*c*) bad for you (complement)

7. A preposition is a word which can precede a noun or pronoun to indicate a relationship between it and other words in a sentence,

e.g. *The book is* **on** *the table.*
They live **outside** *London.*
Your suggestion sounds fine **in** *theory.*

8. A conjunction is a joining word,
e.g. *Girls* **and** *boys*
Although *he's sick he won't stay in bed.*

9. An adjective is a word which describes a noun or pronoun,
e.g. *He's a* **clever** *man.*
The effects of the decision are **far-reaching**.

10. An adverb is a word which modifies an adjective, another adverb, sometimes a preposition, a clause or a phrase,
e.g. *She is* **very** *clever.*
He works **hard**.
They work **extremely hard.**
Basque country is **mostly** *in Spain.*

11. e.g. *told* in: *She told* **the children a story**.

(indirect obj. direct obj.)

B. 1. noun 2. noun 3. verb (intransitive) 4. adjective 5. conjunction 6. preposition 7. pronoun (possessive) 8. verb (intransitive) 9. adverb 10. noun or intransitive verb 11. noun, transitive or intransitive verb 12. adjective 13. transitive verb 14. adjective 15. adverb 16. intransitive verb 17. conjunction 18. noun 19. noun 20. intransitive verb 21. conjunction 22. preposition or adverb 23. noun 24. transitive verb.

C. *Category one (utterances containing transitive verbs) 1, 2, 4, 6, 7, 10*

Category two (utterances containing intransitive verbs) 3, 5, 8, 9

D. 1. his girlfriend
2. her
3. champagne
4. her

5. her
6. him
7. the curtains, the coffee
8. an excuse

E.
1. *because* (a conjunction) is wrongly used as a preposition.
2. Subject pronoun *she* is wrongly used where object pronoun *her* is required.
3. *quickly* (an adverb) is wrongly used as an adjective.
4. *during* (a preposition) is wrongly used as a conjunction.
5. *avoid* (a transitive verb) is wrongly used intransitively.
6. *slow* (an adjective) is wrongly used as an adverb.
7. *given* (3rd person singular form of verb) is wrongly used after 3rd person plural pronoun *they*.
8. *listen* (an intransitive verb) is wrongly used transitively. (A preposition – *to* – is needed to make sense of the utterance.)

F. Because the structure words *he, his, and, out, a, they, until, a, to, them* are all recognisable and give an acceptable framework to the nonsense words, and because some of the nonsense words are marked by their endings as verbs ('crattl**ed**', 'strenter**ed**', 'veen**ed**') or adverbs ('folic**ly**'), or because they sound right in context.

G. Depending on the dictionary, they may or may not appear as headwords. In any case none of them are the obvious forms for a dictionary to list. A verb is normally listed under its infinitive.

SECTION TWO

Commentary

A. All the utterances express habitual or routine actions, signalled in different ways:
1. by the present simple verb
2. by the adjective and noun
3. by the *used to* structure

79

4. by the phrase *in the habit of*
5. by the association of *always* with the verb in the present continuous form.

B. All the utterances contain verbs in the present continuous form, expressing something different each time:
1. an *ongoing* process (over a long undefined period)
2. something happening now (for a short period)
3. an expression of future intention; the meaning here depends on the time adverb *tonight*
4. an habitual action; the meaning here depends on the adverb *always*

C. All the utterances contain or consist of verbs in the imperative forms, expressing something different each time:
1. an instruction
2. an invitation
3. an order
4. a supplication
5. a standard response to thanks
6. advice

D. All the utterances refer to the future, but the verb forms differ and the shades of meaning differ:
1. a parting greeting, short for *I'll see you* which implies that the parties concerned will meet again soon, in the normal course of events
2. part of a pre-arranged programme (futurity expressed by *due to* and the time)
3. an expectation (near future expressed by *about to*)
4. statement about the future (train departure) based on known facts (a regular timetable)
5. expression of intention (*going to . . .*)
6. this could be his intention, or merely a neutral statement of what lies ahead of him – the futurity is expressed only by the time phrase *in June* – note the change of meaning if these words are omitted!
7. this is an unalterable fact about the future – often called the **pure** future, expressed by *shall/will*

E. Each utterance contains an element of hypothesis:
1. a piece of advice; the speaker uses the common device of putting himself in his listener's place
2. . . . but the listener is still there, therefore the *unreal* element
3. . . . but you're not!
4. . . . but he didn't (and so he failed his exams)
5. . . . but no-one did

The verb forms correspond to the subjunctive in many other languages – they *look* like past tense verbs but in meaning are not related to the past. For further treatment of this topic, see Section 7.

F. Each utterance expresses a degree of possibility or probability, differing in degree:
1. very improbably
2. possible
3. self-explanatory
4. certain
5. probable

For a fuller treatment of this topic see Section 7.

SECTION THREE

Commentary

(n.b. Initial trainees may find this exercise puzzling and will need guidance. See G. Leech and J. Svartvik *A Communicative Grammar of English* (Longman) p 74–5 for a diagrammatic representation of tense/time relationships. This is an initial sensitisation exercise; most of the problems raised receive more detailed treatment in subsequent exercises.)

A. (*i*) 3 (*ii*) 7 (*iii*) 1 (*iv*) 2 (*v*) 5 (*vi*) 6 (*vii*) 4

B. 1. Present time is usually expressed by present tenses; present tenses may, however, be used in combination with future time expressions, to express future time.

81

2. This is generally true; the *pastness* is signalled by the form of the verb and the time is specified when necessary, in an adverbial phrase.

3. This certainly is not true, and early attempts to write grammars of English on the lines of Latin grammars resulted in some persistent misunderstandings about how the English verb system works, e.g. over the existence of a future *tense*, and the meanings accorded to various forms of the past.

4. and 5.
American linguists assure us that the Hopi Indians lack time concepts, but as few learners of English live in such social and cultural isolation, it is safe to assume that most speakers of other languages perceive time in much the same ways as we do. Difficulties are caused for the foreign learner less because of perceptual problems than because different languages express time concepts in different ways, e.g. the present perfect in German expresses much of what is expressed in the simple past in English; Chinese has no varying verb forms – time differences are expressed by adverbial particles. (Speakers of Arabic, when speaking of the future, usually add the proviso "God willing", an example of religious belief affecting the way time is perceived and expressed in a language.)

6. Occasionally it is the only time marker, but there is almost always reinforcement in the form of a time adverbial. Thus, speakers of languages with highly inflected verb systems, e.g. French, Spanish, Russian, often underrate the importance of these adverbial phrases and omit them.

SECTION FOUR

Commentary

A. *Category one. Questions requiring* yes *or* no *answers: 3, 5, 7, 9, 11*

Category two. Questions requiring information in the answer: 1, 2, 4, 6, 8, 10, 12

Another possibility would be:

Category one. Questions beginning with a question word: 1, 2, 4, 6, 10, 12

Category two. Questions formed by subject/verb inversion: 3, 5, 7, 8, 9, 11

B. *Category one. Questions asking for information: 1, 5, 9*

Category two. Questions expecting a negative reply: 2, 4, 7 (perhaps!), 11

Category three. Requests: 3, 8

Category four. Questions expecting a positive reply: 6, 7 (perhaps!), 13, 14

Category five. Offers: 10, 12

There are other ways these questions could be grouped, e.g. into those with and those without tail questions. Questions can have many functions and it is not enough merely to teach the rules about inversion and the use of *do/does/did*.

C. 1. Learner has not absorbed the fact that the main verb reverts to infinitive after *do/does/did*. This may only be apparent in the 3rd person singular of the present simple which differs from the infinitive form through the extra *-s.*

2. Learner has not modified the word order. Difficulty arises over the difference between *Aren't I* (a mystery anyway!) and *Am I not.*

3. Same problem as in C1 above, except that the verb is now in the simple past.

4. Learner has failed to absorb the rule about question formation with *do/does*. The chances are that his mother tongue forms questions by direct inversion of subject and main verb.

5. False analogy here. Learner has wrongly applied what

83

he knows about question formation with *do/does* to an auxiliary verb *can*.

6. Learner has chosen the main verb instead of the auxiliary to form the tail question.

7. Learner has not grasped that *shall* in questions is usually only used with the first person singular and plural. The mistake may be one of false analogy; the learner may have heard *Shall I . . .?* and generalised from it.

D. 1. The polite greeting (which normally requires an identical reply) has been mistaken for a genuine enquiry about health.

2. This is a common error! The polite enquiry about health (seldom answered honestly by an Englishman!) has been mistaken for a standard greeting requiring an identical reply.

3. The *can* of the question has been understood to refer to **ability**; in fact the question is a request for assistance. English speakers sometimes **deliberately** misunderstand *can* questions in this way!

4. The question has been mistakenly understood as referring to the present moment; the *do* should be received as a signal denoting a question about habit or routine.

5. The questioner wanted reassurance. The impatient reply shows that the speaker has interpreted the question as expressing lack of confidence in his ability to finish the work.

In each case, the **function** of the question has not been understood, though there is obvious familiarity with the **forms**.

E. Context would dictate appropriate intonation which would in turn give the listener the clue as to the function of each question, but these are the most likely choices.
1e 2a 3h 4b 5f 6c 7d 8i 9j 10g
The exercise demonstrates the vital role of intonation in determining function.

F. 1. Maybe because the **teacher** does too much questioning and does not give his learners sufficient opportunity to initiate communication.

2. The word *interrogative* describes the grammatical form which is used to ask a *question*. The rules for the formation of interrogatives are fairly easily assimilated and can be committed to memory; learners need to know when and how to ask the **question** appropriate to their communicative needs.

SECTION FIVE

Commentary

A. 1. *I'll help* . . . expresses an offer of assistance.

2. **Will** expresses irritation at a bad habit.

3. . . . *will you* . . . expresses a request (familiar or slightly impatient)

4. *Shall I* . . . expresses an offer of assistance.

5. This is **pure future**.

6. *Shall we* . . . expresses a suggestion.

7. This one is marginal. It may be seen as **pure future** or as expressing inevitability (to be interpreted as a threat or warning).

8. *will* . . . expresses the resigned attitude of the speaker to a universally accepted state of affairs.

9. *will* is required after *think* in a request for an opinion about the future.

10. *shall* expresses insistence, the imposing of an obligation.

11. This is **pure future**.

One of the points of this exercise is to show how comparatively rarely *shall* and *will* are used with **pure future** meaning, which means that it could be very confusing to refer to them as **the future tense**.

B. The examples show how rarely we talk completely dispassionately about the future. The past is the past and can't be changed. When we talk about the future, however, we often express ourselves personally – in this exercise there are examples of expressions of hope, probability, intention and possibility as well as the neutral future expressed in 1 and 9.

C. Some teachers would teach *shall/will* first as it is most commonly identified as, and associated with, the future.

Others would go for the present continuous plus time adverb as this does not entail learning a new structure. *Going to* also has the present continuous form and is useful in expresssions of intention and probability. Choice of which to teach first will depend on many factors, e.g. mother tongue of learners, the type of English they need, etc.

D. 1. Not acceptable. *Shall* is seldom used in normal **statements** in spoken English as the short forms *I'll* and *We'll* are preferred. But it is still needed in interrogative forms *Shall I . . .?* and *Shall we . . .?*

2. Not acceptable. *Will* is, in fact, often used with first persons, and *shall* can be used with the second person to express insistence (You **shall** do it!).

3. Acceptable, with the exception of interrogatives, for reasons stated in **D**1 above.

4. Grammar books are inevitably behind the times. There are still teachers of English who **insist** on *shall* in all first person statements, but to do this is to ignore trends in the language.

5. *Shall* should be taught when it is needed, i.e. to help in the expression of suggestions (*Shall we go for a walk?*) and offers of help (*Shall I open it for you?*), but not merely for the sake of formal completeness when the future is being taught.

The majority of these statements also apply to *should* and *would*, though it is worth noting that *should* is very commonly used to give advice or impose obligations (e.g. *You should see a doctor* or *You should work harder*).

SECTION SIX

Commentary

A. In shop windows, restaurants etc. in tourist areas. French, German and Spanish all use **active** constructions with impersonal forms. English uses the passive. This is typical of the preference English has for the passive in impersonal expressions.

B. 1. Notice (*written*) in a supermarket. Use of passive shows that it is written, not spoken. Word *customers* comes first to catch the eye.

2. Car owner contacting police or talking to someone about theft of his car. Car dominates his thoughts and is mentioned first. Name of thief not known and not relevant to what the owner wants to express at this stage.

3. News bulletin or newspaper article. The high number of people is shocking and comes first. The passive helps to emphasise this; at this stage, the name of the person who **reported** this is irrelevant.

4. Reply to a question like *Where's your car?* Name of person repairing the car is irrelevant here; interest centres on the car.

5. Admonition to make sure the listener knows the consequences of an action he has planned. The use of the passive adds formality, weight and distance to the statement.

6. Notice. (*e.g. on building site, private estate*) No-one is interested in who does the prosecuting – the emphasis is on the fate awaiting trespassers.

7. Newspaper headline. Name of assassin probably not yet known and Kennedy is the focal point of the article.

C. It is written too loosely and informally. The title is *Oxygen* and this should generally be the subject. It could be rewritten as follows:

Oxygen

Oxygen was first prepared by Joseph Priestley in 1774. He prepared it by heating mercuric oxide but nowadays it is produced commercially in large quantities by a process called fractional distillation. It is contained in both air and water and is given off by plants in their respiratory process. (The use of the passive ensures focus on *Oxygen* as the central theme and cuts down on the number of repetitions of 'it', which makes the original version sound so clumsy.)

D. The exercise is futile because (*a*) there is no communicative point in turning active sentences into the passive and (**b**) the passive is simply not appropriate to all the examples, especially nos. 1 and 2.

It also encourages production of tautologous examples like

Our house was broken into *by somebody* last night

The **agent** is superfluous here as (presumably) animals and birds do not burgle houses!

E. 1. The first one implies that boredom drove them home. The second one implies that all work had been completed and there was nothing more in need of attention.

  2. The first one implies that Scotland offers little interest to the visitor. The second one implies that the streets are empty of people.

F. All are in the passive but none has a normally used active form, a fact made clearer in each case by the absence of an **agent**.

G. 1. The passive formalises and depersonalises the warning.

  2. The passive lets the P.M. off the hook. Politicians often use it to avoid the consequences of being directly quoted – in this example the P.M. expresses optimism without giving the required undertaking which he might later regret.

  3. The passive allows the spokesman to make a non-committal statement, designed to discourage further questioning.

  4. The professor's use of the passive focuses attention on the real author and emphasises the student's mistake to him.

  5. Fred is able to take up his questioner's interest in Joe by choosing the passive, which allows Joe to remain the subject of the sentence.

H. 1. Choice allows emphasis on the **patient** (i.e. the person or thing affected by an action) – which is often at the centre of interest in news stories e.g. – *Embassy occupied, Everton defeated, Carter snubbed.*

2. See **G2** above – the passive allows politicians to be suitably non-committal and may enable them to avoid being quoted later.

3. In scientific reports, the emphasis is usually on **what** is done, not **who** does it. Thus when experiments are written up, the passive is preferred – e.g. *A test-tube was taken and half-filled with copper sulphate solution. It was then heated over a moderate flame . . . etc.*
No-one is interested in **who** does this.

In normal colloquial speech, there is usually less call for detachment and objectivity. The passive adds formality, another element not usually required in colloquial speech.

I. 1. In the first sentence, he paid someone to do it for him; in the second sentence, he did it himself.

2. In the first sentence, the subject wants to pay someone to develop the film for him. The second sentence is a more neutral question and does not necessarily imply an immediate desire for the service.

3. There is a shift of emphasis here, too. The first one implies an arrangement with the dentist; the second is a simple statement of fact.

J. The sentences would need to be completed on these lines:
1. *. . . do you have it cut?*
2. *. . . do you have it done?*
3. *. . . do you have it delivered?*
4. *. . . do you have them made?*
5. *. . . do you have it cleaned?*

As an exercise requiring some initiative, it is acceptable. As a drill, it falls down as the information in the first part is not always adequate to allow correct completion.

SECTION SEVEN

Commentary

A. The verb forms in **bold** type all have the appearance of past tenses (with the exception of *would rain* in the first sentence), but do not carry any past meaning. In fact they all express something hypothetical, and are better termed **subjunctive** forms than past tense forms as the use of the word *past* in this connection is confusing. The subjunctive is obvious only in the first person of 'to be' (*If I were . . .*) as in no. 4.

B. 1 (*b*) 2 (*c*) 3 (*a*)

C. 1 and 9 – *would* as past form of *will* to maintain sequence of tenses after *think* and *was hoping*.
2, 4, 6, 10 – all have an element of hypothesis.
3 and 8 – *would* makes the requests sound polite.
5 and 7 – *would* expresses habit – it is typical of you to forget your keys, and of Queen Victoria to smile very seldom.

There are other possible groupings, but these suffice to show the wide range of meaning of *would* as an auxiliary. The terms *conditional tense* and *conditional sentences* are common headings in grammars and course books. But there is no real conditional tense in English, only expressions of conditional or hypothetical meaning. It is more useful to speak of conditional **sentences** though textbooks often confusingly refer to a sequence of tenses in sentences such as nos. 4 and 8, insisting that a **conditional tense** must be used in the main clause whereas the verb in the subordinate clause should be in the **past tense**. It is almost certainly easier for foreign learners to become familiar with *would* as a commonly used auxiliary with many different meanings, one of which is to express conditions.

D. *Group one: 2, 4, 6, 11, 12 (possibly) – all express developments which are certain to take place if a condition is fulfilled – and there seems a strong likelihood in each instance that the condition* **will** *be fulfilled.*

Group two: 1, 5, 7, 9, 12 (possibly), 13 – all express much more unlikely developments as the condition in each case is unlikely to be fulfilled. In sentence 1, the speaker seems unlikely to have more time, in sentence 5, the speaker can never actually change his identity, in sentence 7, the speaker is clearly not terribly optimistic about the chances of his friend giving up smoking, etc. etc.

Group three: 3, 8, 10 – all these deal with the past. In each case the speaker or writer looks back on a past event and states a condition on which things would have turned out differently. It's too late to alter the course of these past events.

Incidentally, these examples show that *if* is certainly not the only conjunction used in conditions.

SECTION EIGHT

Commentary

A.
1. To indicate that the action was recent and is of current relevance.
2. *a)* Suggestion. *b)* Suggestion or instruction.
3. Indicates past action and contributes to the formal, impersonal tenor of the utterance.
4. Seeking confirmation of what is hoped for or expected.
5. Indicates purpose.
6. Polite request.
7. Coordination and sequence.
8. Indicates future arrangement.
9. Linking two apparently incompatible sentences.
10. Indicating reference back to a house specified in a previous utterance.
11. Contributing to a reasoned refusal or indicating reluctance.
12. Referring back to a previously mentioned topic.
13. Referring to action at a particular point of time in the past.

14. Indicating reaction to a frequent habit.
15. Coordination and addition.
16. Expressing polite or qualified disagreement.

B. *Function* = job; role; what the word or phrase does in the utterance.

C. 1. *Function* = the purpose of the utterance, i.e. what the speaker/writer intends to achieve through the utterance (e.g. invite somebody; indicate disagreement).
   Examples: 1 *b*); 2; 4; 6; 11; 14; 16.
2. *Function* = the information conveyed through the structure (e.g. the time reference).
   Examples: 1 *a*); 3; 5; 7; 8; 9; 13; 15.
3. *Function* = the grammatical role of the utterance (e.g. reference back to a previous expression; joining two expressions).
   Examples: 7; 9; 10; 12; 15.

Function 2 is related to **what** the speaker/hearer says whereas Function 1 is related to **why** he says it.

D. The potential information of the structure (i.e. Function 2).

E. It relates to the purposes of utterances (i.e. Function 1).

F. 1. *A* Suggestion
      B Refusal
   2. *A* Indicating conviction
      B Indicating strong disagreement
   3. *A* Invitation
      B Acceptance
   4. *A* Instruction
      B Query
   5. *A* Advice
      B Agreement

SECTION NINE

Commentary

A. 1. They are all ways of expressing disagreement.

2. *a)*

Formal	Semi-Formal	Informal
4, 5, 10, 12	1, 2, 3, 5, 7, 9, 10, 12, 15	3, 5, 6, 8, 9, 12 14, 15

b)

Strong	Definite	Tentative
8, 13, 14	2, 3, 4, 5, 9, 10, 11, 12	1, 2, 6, 7, 15

c)

Factual statements	Opinions
6, 8, 9, 12, 13, 14	1, 2, 3, 4, 5, 6, 7, 8, 10, 11, 12, 13, 14, 15

d)

Initiating	Responding
6, 10, 15	1–15

3. It is important to differentiate between the different exponents of a function and vital that the learner does not regard them as interchangeable.

B. 1. The students are merely repeating exponents that they have been taught. They are making no attempt to select the most appropriate exponents and they are disregarding each others' utterances. They are practising the forms of the exponents but they are certainly not practising their use.

2. The teacher probably listed the exponents of complaining together and the exponents of apologising together. He then probably concentrated on getting students to produce the correct forms of the exponents through imitation and substitution drills. He might have exemplified the exponents in situations but he certainly has not succeeded in teaching that the exponents are not interchangeable and that each exponent is subtly different from the others. He has probably also encouraged the students to get as many exponents into their dialogue as possible and has not encouraged them to restrict the exponents they use to those that are appropriate to the situation and to the other participants' utterances. When the students performed their *impromptu* dialogue they could probably see a list of exponents on the board or on a chart.

93

3. 1. Restrict the exponents you teach.
    2. Differentiate between the exponents in your teaching.
    3. Set up practice situations which encourage the learners to select the exponents appropriate to the situation and to the utterances of the other participant(s).

C. 1. It is not real because it consists of a series of interchanges each consisting of request/refusal and each unconnected with the others. It seems to have been designed to practise or elicit as many exponents of request and refusal as possible and ends up giving the impression that the exponents are interchangeable.

There is no consistency of tenor (e.g. the requests range from very polite to very rude) and the responses are often totally inappropriate (e.g. a very polite request eliciting a very rude refusal) and the *tone* is often inappropriate to what is being requested (e.g. *I'd be so grateful if you could find your way to lending me a pen for a minute*).

2. 1. Requests
    2. Refusal

3. 1. *Requests*

Very polite	*Polite*	*Impolite*
I'd be so grateful	Please could	How about – ing
if you could	you	Give me . . .
possibly find	possibly . . .	
your way to . . .		

2. *Reluctant*

1. | *Reluctant* | *Definite* |
    |---|---|
    | I wish I could but . . . | I'm broke |
    | If only I could | No way |

2. | *Reason given* | *No reason given* |
    |---|---|
    | I'm broke | No way |
    | . . . it's in the garage | |
    | If only I could | |

5. The important criteria for selection are:
    1. coverage (i.e. the ability of an exponent to be used instead of others) e.g. *Could you please . . . me . . .*

could cover all the other exponents of polite requests.

2. frequency (i.e. how often an exponent is used in everyday situations)
3. context frequency (i.e. how often an exponent is used in particular situations)
4. learnability (i.e. how easy the exponent is to learn), e.g. *Could you please... me...* is easier to learn than *I'd be so grateful if you could possibly find your way to ...*

N.B. 1. The more exponents that are taught at once the greater is the danger of confusion.
2. Some exponents should be selected for students to learn to understand and to use; others should be selected only for them to learn to respond to when they are exposed to them.

SECTION TEN

Commentary

A. Much depends on the intonation and on the context, but all of these appear possible:
ordering, warning, requesting, persuading, begging, advising, recommending, reminding, insisting, suggesting
... and maybe some of the others, too.

B. She ordered   him to take his watch off before jumping in.
warned
requested
tried to persuade
begged
advised
reminded

She suggested   that he should take his watch off before
insisted   jumping in.
recommended

Note that the function is clearer in indirect speech, a

feature mainly of written English, which is denied the extra dimensions of gesture, facial expression, stress and intonation all of which help to signal the meaning of a spoken utterance.

C. Following on from the conclusions in the previous exercise, it is clearly difficult to decide on the **functions** of many of the ten utterances, and therefore to choose an appropriate expression in indirect speech. In any case, there is no communicative point to the exercise as it stands. When indirect speech is used in written English, it is most often in connected prose and the exercise consists of ten unrelated examples giving no practice in connected writing.

SECTION ELEVEN

Commentary

A. 1. They all communicate aspects of the notion of duration of time (i.e. they refer to periods of time).

    2. 1. To refer to a complete period of time with either past, present or future time reference. Always followed by an expression referring to a period of time.

        2. See example.

        3. To refer to a period of time from a point previously mentioned (or indicated in the situation) to the point of time mentioned immediately after *till* – Can be used with past, present or future time reference and always followed by an expression referring to a point of time.

        4. As for 3.

        5. To refer to a lengthy and uninterrupted period of time. Can have past, present or future time reference.

        6. To refer to what happened continuously during a period of time in the past.

        7. To refer to what happened continuously during a period of time in the past between two indicated points of time.

8. To indicate that a question is being asked about the length of an indicated period of time in the past or future.

9. To refer to all of a previously indicated period of time in the past, present or future.

10. To indicate the length of a period of time in the past or future.

11. To indicate that the opinion is constant.

B. 1. They all communicate aspects of the notion of movement.

2. 1. *moved* – indicates movement.
   slowly – indicates speed of movement.
   forward – indicates direction of movement from the starting point.

   2. Indicates intended *terminus* of movement.

   3. Indicates movement from outside to inside.

   4. *walking* – indicates means of movement.
   towards – indicates direction of movement by reference to a potential *terminus*.

   5. Indicates movement from inside to outside.

   6. *ran* – indicates means of movement.
   away – indicates movements which achieve distance.
   from – indicates direction of movement by reference to the starting point.

   7. *go* refers to movement from *here*.
   fetch refers to movement from *here* to *there* and then back to *here* again.

4. One possible answer would be:
   1. means of movement
   to walk; to run; to swim; to drive; to travel.

   2. Speed of movement
   slowly; quickly.

   3. Direction of movement
   1 to
   2 forward(s); backward(s); sideward(s).
   3 towards; away; from.
   4 into; out of; out.

97

C. 1. e.g. *1 The mouse was inside this cupboard.*
          2 This is where we will meet on Friday.
          3 It's on that table.
  2. Relative position.
  3. Sequence.

D. 1. *1.* Manner
    2. Result
    3. Comparison
    4. Instrument
    5. Time
  2. e.g. *Time*
    1. *then* = immediately after the previous occurrence mentioned *e.g. I put the money in the safe. Then I rang the manager.*
    2. *meanwhile* = at approximately the same time as the previous occurrence mentioned.
       e.g. Mr Carter was operated on at 2 p.m. Meanwhile his brother was standing by to give blood if it was required.
    3. *whilst* = at the same time as the previous occurrence mentioned was taking place.
       e.g. I papered the living room whilst my wife painted the kitchen.

N.B.

Whilst relates two continuous actions together in time and usually in place. It joins two clauses (or a clause and a phrase within one sentence).

Meanwhile relates two events together in time and type. It links two sentences together.

e.g. *I listened to the radio whilst peeling the potatoes.*
  x *I listened to the radio. Meanwhile I peeled the potatoes. So England were convincing winners of the European Championship. Meanwhile in Lima last night Brazil beat Peru to win the South American Championship.*
  x *So England were convincing winners of the European Championship whilst in Lima last night Brazil beat Peru to win the South American Championship.*

SECTION TWELVE

Commentary

A. 1.*a* 2.*a* 3.*b* 4.*a* 5.*b* 6.*b* 7.*a* 8.*b* 9.*a* 10.*b* 11.*b* 12.*b* 13.*b* 14.*b* 15.*b*

B. The boundaries on the *pie* chart are obviously arbitrary. There are no **right** answers here, and there is certain to be disagreement about which segment some of the sentences belong in. This is, in itself, a warning **against** attempts to pin down differences between fine shades of meaning. Here, **for guidance only**, is one possible interpretation.
1.I 2.F 3.E 4.D 5.A 6.G 7.H 8.B 9.B 10.G 11.C 12.G 13.B 14.H 15.G

There are many views about which sentence types to teach first, but one approach would be to choose three or four points on the scale between *out of the question* and *absolute certainty* and to select the commonest ways of expressing these degrees of meaning. It is worth noting that modal meaning is expressed in many different ways, not just by the use of modal auxiliaries. The simplest way, structurally, is by the addition of a single adverb such as *perhaps*, *maybe* or *definitely*.

C. They are distinguished by their relative formality or informality. The question of which to teach first ought to be decided by the learners' priorities and the circumstances in which they are most likely to be using English. The most neutral choice is probably *Can I go home now?* though 'Could I . . .' adds a touch of extra politeness (often an asset for foreigners in an English-speaking environment!)

D. 1. Expresses likelihood.
2. Expresses discontinued ability.
3. Asks permission.
4. Expresses absence of obligation.
5. Expresses disapproval or disappointment at failure to do something.
6. Expresses logical impossibility.
7. Expresses logical certainty.

8.   Gives permission.
9.   Expresses possibility.
10. Expresses obligation.

E.   There are many different ways of expressing each of these. Two or three are given here in each case to ensure that the basic concept is clear:

1.   He *may possibly* come.
     Perhaps he'll come.
     There's *a chance that* he'll come.
2.   She's *capable* of defending herself.
     She *can* defend herself.
     She *has the ability* to defend herself.
3.   You *must* help your father.
     You're *obliged to* help your father.
     It's *your responsibility* to help your father.
4.   You *have to* have a cholera injection if you travel to the Middle East.
     A cholera injection *is required* for travel to the Middle East.
     You *need* a cholera injection if you travel to the Middle East.
5.   He *will* keep grinding his teeth.
     He's *always* grinding his teeth.

In all the examples, note once again how many ways there are of expressing modality other than by auxiliaries.

F.   1.   *could* is reserved for general ability in the past.
     was able is used with the meaning of *managed to* (usually on a single occasion) but also to express general ability.
     e.g. *He could* ⎱ *swim well when he was younger.*
           was able to ⎰
     but *He was able to escape by swimming the river.*
     Could would not be possible in the second example.
2.   Compare these examples to understand the difference:
     You mustn't drink that! It's poison. (mother to child)
     You don't have to drink that tea. It's gone cold. (host to guest)
     The first utterance prohibits. The second one removes obligation.

100

3. Compare these examples:
   You should eat less.
   You ought to eat less.
   We use *should* and *ought to* to impose moral obligations
   and they are practically interchangeable, though *ought
   to* is arguably more forceful.

4. Compare these examples:
   You don't need to pay now.
   You needn't pay now.
   There is no significant difference.

5. *I may come* is more likely than I *might come.*

6. Modal auxiliaries modify the meaning of the verb they
   are linked to. Ordinary auxiliaries, e.g. *have, is, do, did*
   simply change the tense, the aspect or the interrogative/
   affirmative/negative status of the verb form.

7. *shall* is used mainly in first person forms, to offer
   assistance: *Shall I do that for you?*, to make a suggestion:
   Shall we go now?, or in *pure* future statements,
   interchangeable with *will.*

   I shall ⎫
   will ⎭ be 64 next birthday.

   will is used with all other persons in *pure* future
   expressions, but also to express willingness: *Will you
   help me?*; promises: *I will* (in marriage ceremony); offers
   of help: *I'll do it for you,* and bad habits: *Joe will talk
   with his mouth full.*

   Foreign learners who have been taught by non-native
   speakers often make too much of the difference between
   shall and *will* in future statements. In fact, the elided
   forms, *I'll, we'll, you'll* etc. often make the difference
   irrelevant. (See also Unit 2, Section 5)

8. Compare these examples:
   John used to smoke.
   *When I was a boy my grandfather used to/would take
   me on his knee and tell me stories.*
   The first example, in which only *used to* is feasible,
   expresses a single discontinued habit. The second
   example, in which either *used to* or *would* is possible,

expresses one of a number of events or experiences bracketed by a time reference (in this case 'When I was a boy' is the time reference).

SECTION THIRTEEN

Commentary

A. Those underlined twice are main verbs; they contribute meaning to their utterances. Those underlined once are not the main verbs in their clauses; their function is to *help* the main verbs to contribute meaning or to add to the meaning of the main verbs.

B. Those underlined twice are main verbs whereas those underlined once are verbs helping main verbs.

C. 1. Those underlined twice are verbs which add to the meaning of the main verb. They usually indicate something about the attitude or opinion of the speaker and are called modal verbs.

   Those underlined once help the main verbs and are called auxiliary verbs.

   Both types of verbs can be used to:
   1. form the interrogative
   2. form the negative
   3. stand for the main verb in short form responses (e.g. 5 and 10)
   4. stand for the main verb in question tags
   In addition those underlined once (i.e. auxiliary verbs) are used to help form tenses and to help indicate number and person (e.g. *I have been/ He has been; he is playing/ they are playing*).

   2. Other modal verbs are:

   should   has to
   will   might
   would   dare

D. 1. **has** = helping to form the present perfect tense of the

main verb (. . . an auxiliary)
2. **had to** = adding to the meaning of the main verb (. . . a modal)
3. **have** = main verb.

E. 1. Helping to form the tense of the main verb.
   2. Forming the negative of the main verb.
   3. Forming the interrogative of the main verb.
   4. Standing for the main verb in:
      1. short form answers
      2. short form responses
      3. question tags.
   5. Helping to indicate the person of the subject (i.e. first, second or third).
   6. Helping to indicate the number of the subject (i.e. singular or plural).

F. 1. *1.* was
       2. wasn't
       3. had
       4. was
       5. did
       6. did
       7. did
       8. were
       9. had
       10. was
       11. did
       12. had
   2. *1.* Yes. To help the past continuous tense and to help form the interrogative.
      2. Yes. To form the negative and to stand for the main verb.
      3. Yes. To help form the past perfect tense.
      4. No.
      5. Yes. To help form the interrogative and the past simple tense.
      6. Yes. To stand for the main verb and to indicate the past simple tense.

7. Yes. As for 6.

8. No.

9. No.

10. Yes. To help form the past continuous tense.

11. Yes. To stand for the main verb (take) and to indicate the past simple tense.

12. Yes. To help form the past perfect tense.

SECTION FOURTEEN

Commentary

A. Suggestions only. Many alternatives are possible, but note the verb forms.

1. 'When did the 'phone ring?'
2. 'What were you doing when the 'phone rang?'
3. 'Have you got the time?'/'Have you finished yet?'
4. 'Did you have a good time at the circus?'
5. 'Has he got two brothers?'/'He's got two brothers, hasn't he?'
6. 'What did you have for breakfast this morning?'
7. 'What sort of car have you got?'
8. 'What are you doing?'
9. 'Have you ever been to Japan?'
10. 'You're having a check-up soon, aren't you?'
11. 'What have they had, a boy or a girl?'
12. 'Have you got a light, please?'

B.
1. *have* here has causative force. Someone is taking his tonsils out **for** him, possibly at his request (See also Unit 2. Section 6. Ex I & J).
2. The assumption is that the person addressed is not always cruel and is capable of changing his behaviour.
3. *has* here is a substitute for the (slightly) tautologous *eat*. The verb has positive, dynamic force.
4. . . . but in a while she'll come to her senses, change her behaviour and be sensible again.
5. *have* here means *accept*.
6. Again, there is causative force here. She has instructed someone to perm her hair for her.

104

7. Present continuous passive: *being repainted* – stresses the fact that the process is under way at the time of speaking. *Be* as a passive auxiliary has a dynamic force.

C. *1(b)* is unacceptable as *handsome* is a **stative** adjective (it describes a permanent state, in contrast to *careful*, which describes a temporary state).

2(b) is unacceptable. (a) is an admonition which applies to a single instance and is in the imperative. There is no obvious **behaviour** which is identifiable as 'being late' and so this is not acceptable here.

3(b) is unacceptable for similar reasons to those stated in *1* and *2*. Stubbornness may be a permanent trait of character but the statement *She's being stubborn* clearly describes her behaviour in a particular instance. The adjective 'beautiful' describes permanent appearance rather than passing behaviour, which makes the continuous form inappropriate.

4(a) is unacceptable. *Have* with the meaning of *possess* cannot be used in the continuous form. In *4(b) having* expresses an activity; it could (unlike *4(a)*) answer the question *What are you doing?*

5(b) is unacceptable. You can't **offer** someone a headache!

6(b) is unacceptable in most contexts. The use of *just* plus present perfect usually indicates a recently completed action, as in *6(a)*.

7(b) is unacceptable in most contexts. *Being British* is not (unless in a mime or charade!) a temporary state of affairs. The use of the present participle in *7(a)* is a normal way of introducing a cause/effect relationship in an utterance.

8(b) would normally not be acceptable. *Has got* is usually used to express possession as in *8(a)* though it could also be used in utterances like *She's got an appointment*, though this would normally refer only to a single instance; the addition of *every evening* in *8(b)* adds an extra dimension.

9(b) is clearly unacceptable. Whilst *have*, in its dynamic sense, forms questions and negatives with the auxiliary *do, be* does not. The correct version of *9(b)* would be simply *I'm not always stupid.*

D. *Category one (dynamic uses): 1, 3, 8, 9, 10, 11, 12*

Category two (stative uses): 2, 4, 5, 6, 7, 13, 14
N.B. In 4 and 6 the stupidity is seen as a permanent characteristic; in 8 it is seen as a temporary state.

E. **Be** is used as an auxiliary in 1 and 5 (twice).
Have is used as an auxiliary in 2, 3¹, 7¹ and 9.

F. 1. This is a common misconception, particularly amongst overseas teachers anxious to avoid *slang. Have got* is absolutely standard in spoken English, and should be taught; it is usually avoided in formal **written** English.

2. The foreign learner has clearly picked up the auxiliary from the command in his short response. He may have been trained to listen for the auxiliary in **questions** to enable him to make the correct short response, but is not yet aware that this does not apply to imperatives. (The fact that the example contains *be* is a distractor here – it could equally well have been *Don't go* or *Don't speak*).

3. The foreign learner has either been told to avoid *got* or has wrongly used the negative form appropriate to the auxiliary *have*, when this *have* expresses possession.

4. Perhaps the main conclusion is that **be** and **have** have to be *recycled* at intervals. Attention then has to be drawn to the distinct meanings and their grammatical consequences. It is significant that there *is no dynamic use of* **be** and **have** in most other languages:

cf. *He's having breakfast.*
Er frühstückt gerade. (German)
Il prend son petit déjeuner. (French)
She's being silly.
Sie spinnt. (German)
Elle fait des bêtises. (French)

SECTION FIFTEEN

Commentary

A. All of them contain implicit or explicit comparisons or contrasts usually between two ideas or objects.

1. Expresses a straightforward comparison (of. length) between two rivers.
2. Expresses a contrast between two cars; an explanation of one aspect in which they differ.
3. Expresses a contrast between two types of coal.
4. A direct comparison of intelligence between Willy and his brother, this time expressed negatively.
5. There is an implicit contrast and comparison between the two flats.
6. A comparison of hair colour, revealing *sameness* rather than *difference*.
7. . . . that is, more clearly than you are doing! A comparison between the present way of speaking and the wished-for way.
8. A comparison of character between two brothers, using a noun *extrovert* rather than a descriptive adjective.
9. A comparison of membership numbers between the *A.A.* and other motoring organisations.
10. Comparison between an actual and an ideal state of affairs.
11. A comparison between degrees of happiness as a way of setting an ideal to aim at.
12. This is almost a platitude which equates an increase in enjoyment. The comparison is proportionate.
13. A comparison for effect, between existing weather conditions and *ice*, representing the ultimate in cold.
14. Another platitude, comparing an achievement with an optimum standard.

There are, as these examples show, many ways of expressing comparison and contrast, and it is not sufficient to deal with the topic under the restricted structural heading (common in textbooks) *Comparative and superlative of adjectives and adverbs.*

B. (a) This exercise provides practice in the comparative and

107

superlative **forms** of adjectives without giving any consideration to the function of comparing or to different ways of comparing.

(b) Foreign learners can learn about the different ways of forming the comparative of adjectives.

1. heavy → heavier (two syllables, ending in –y, of easy, happy, etc.)
2. difficult → more difficult (more than two syllables. cf intelligent, important)
3. old → older (monosyllabic adjective cf young, long, short)
4. careful → more careful (two or more syllables, compound adjective cf beautiful, helpful, thoughtless etc.)
5. fast → faster (monosyllabic adverb of hard)
6. obedient → more obedient (cf 2 above)
7. high → highest (superlative of monosyllabic adjective cf short, long, wide)
8. beautiful → most beautiful (superlative of compound adjectives, two or more syllables. cf thoughtful, plentiful)
9. far → farther/further (irregular comparative form)
10. bad → worse (irregular comparative form)

SECTION SIXTEEN

Commentary

A. 1. **got** = past simple = indicating action at a specific time and place in the past.
    had gone = past perfect = indicating action which occurred before the other action referred to.
2. **was walking** = past continuous = indicating continuous action in the past.
    saw = simple past = indicating event at a specific time and place in the past.
3. **will have finished** = future perfect = indicating future event which will have finished before another event (mentioned in the utterance or indicated in the situation) takes place.

have finished = present perfect = indicating action which will occur after another action in the future.

4. **you're** = simple present = indicating present state.
   's gone home = present perfect = indicating action in recent past with present relevance.

5. **see** = indicating present state.
   got arrested = simple past = indicating action at specific time in the past.

6. **walked** = simple past = indicating habitual action in the past.
   worked = simple past = indicating period of time in the past.

7. **comes** = simple present = indicating future action.
   will let . . . know = future simple (or modal + main verb) = indicating present decision about a future action.

8. **does leave** = simple present = indicating usual routine.
   's gone = present perfect = indicating an event in the recent past with present relevance.

9. **'ve been waiting** = present perfect continuous = indicating an event with continuation from a point in the past to the present.

10. **meet** = simple present = indicating past formal arrangement about the future.

11. **has come** = present perfect = indicating an action in the recent past with current relevance.

B.
1. From the choice of the past perfect and from *already*.
2. It would indicate that the walking only started after Mary had been seen.
3. (a) Because of the convention of *will* not being used in time clauses unless it is used to indicate willingness.
   (b) No.
   (c) Yes. It would indicate that a regular state of affairs is being referred to.
4. No. The *just* and the *too late* indicate recent past and suggest present relevance.
5. *See* could be put into the simple past without seriously interfering with the message; *has got arrested* would be grammatically wrong but reference to a specific past action would still be indicated by yesterday.

6. The *every day* and the *when* are strong enough to indicate past habit even if an inappropriate tense was used.

   e.g. **x** *He has walked to work every day when he worked at the station in 1968.*

7. No. The use of the simple present in time clauses with future relevance is a convention. The future reference would still be communicated by the *will let* even if other tenses were used.

   e.g. **x** *When he will come I will let you know.*

   x *When he came I will let you know.*

8. No. Pointing to the departing train is sufficient to indicate recent past and present relevance regardless of the tense used.

   e.g. **x** *It just went.*

   x *It had just gone.*

9. Yes. The present perfect (i.e. I've waited here for thirty minutes).

10. (a) That a formal arrangement has already been made.
    (b) That the arrangement is for a specific time in the future.

11. Not very important. The *yet* is strong enough to indicate recent past and present relevance.

C. 1. . . . change the meaning . . .

   2. . . . function . . . another expression . . . something in the situation.

   3. . . . meaning of the utterance . . . utterance . . . situation . . . meaning . . . clear . . . appropriacy . . . function . . . cause the utterance to be misunderstood.

D.

1	2	3
was walking (2)	got (1)	have finished (3)
're late (4)	had gone (1)	's gone home (4)
will let know (7)	saw (2)	got arrested (5)
does leave (8)	will have finished (3)	worked (6)
meet (10)	see (5)	comes (7)
	walked (6)	's gone (8)
	've been waiting (9)	has come (11)

H. 2. **had slept** – the selection of the past perfect is crucial as it is the only indicator that the child no longer slept there.

3. **had been shifted** – the selection of the past perfect is crucial as it is the only indicator that the shifting took place before the arrival of the writer.

4. **called** – the choice of the past simple is important as it helps to indicate that the room had not been called that before. However the crucial word is *now* and its force could survive an erroneous choice of tense.

5. **lay** – the tense contrasts with the past perfect of the previous sentence and indicates that this was true at that particular time in the past that the writer is describing. However the past continuous, the present simple or the present continuous could have been used without changing the meaning of the utterance.

6. **had . . . succeeded** – the choice of the past perfect again indicates that this happened before the time that is being described.

7. **was lying** – the choice of the past continuous indicates that this was true at the time the writer is describing. However the simple past could have been used without interfering with the grammar or the meaning of the utterance. The simple present and present continuous would have been ungrammatical in contrast with the past perfect but would nevertheless have communicated the same meaning.

I. 1. **it is** – the simple present indicates it is true now. No other tense could have been used.

2. **'s been** – the present perfect indicates that this has been true from a point in the past until now. The simple past could also have been used.

3. **'ve been looking** – the present perfect continuous indicates a continuous action from a point of time in the past until now. The past continuous could have been used with the same function and the simple past and the present perfect, although not grammatically appropriate in this utterance, could have been used without interfering with the message being communicated.

4. **'ll take** – this indicates that a decision is being made now about the future. No other tense would be grammatically acceptable but the situation would probably make this clear if any other tense with potential future reference was used.

5. **'m meeting** – the present continuous indicates that an arrangement has been made in the past for the future. The situation and the *at nine* make the future reference clear but the tense is crucial as an indication of previous arrangement.

6. **'ll give** – as for 4.

7. **was going** – the past continuous indicates a past intention for the future which no longer applies. No other tense could have been used without interfering with the meaning of the utterance.

8. **'s ringing** – the present continuous is used to indicate present duration. No other tense would be grammatically acceptable but the situational signal (i.e. the actual ringing) is so strong that the meaning of the utterance would still be clear if other tenses were used by mistake.

9. **'ll get** – this indicates a present decision about the immediate future. Again the situational signals are so strong that effective communication would probably take place whatever tense was used.

10. **rings** – the simple present is used to indicate that this is a habit. However *usually* and *about this time* are such strong signals of habit that the choice of an inappropriate tense would probably not interfere with communication.

11. **'s stopped** – the present perfect indicates the recent past. However the situation would probably make the meaning clear regardless of what tense was used.

12. **didn't answer** – the simple past refers to a point of time in the past. The situation would allow the inappropriate present perfect and even the incorrect past perfect to be used without serious danger of misapprehension.

J. The following points could be made:
1. The learners do not have to be able to use all the tenses to

112

communicate all their functions as often more than one tense can be used to communicate the same function in the same situation.

2. It is important when teaching the function of a tense to exemplify the use of that tense in utterances which would not permit other tenses to be used and still communicate the same meaning (e.g. the past perfect should be exemplified in utterances in which it is not interchangeable with the simple past).

3. Often the learner can get away with using the wrong tense if his intended function is communicated by other features of the utterance (e.g. *just, usually, often, tomorrow, for, yet, already, every day*). Considerable teaching time should be devoted to those items (mainly adverbials) which can reinforce and sometimes even replace the functional signals of tense.

4. The teacher should be selective in his correction of tense error. Those errors which frustrate communication (e.g. *I had given it to him when you told me to* instead of, *I gave it to him when you told me to*) are more serious than those which do not (e.g. x *I'll tell you before the lesson* **will** *finish*).

SECTION SEVENTEEN

Commentary

A. *Category one (single events or repeated actions): 1, 4, 5.*

Category two (actions spanning a named or implied point in time): 2, 3, 6.

B. 1. The question aims to elicit the learner's reaction to the telephone ringing. He misunderstands it as an enquiry about what he *was doing* when it rang. He is not sensitive to the clearly stated **simple** aspect of the question 'What *did* you *do* . . .?' This is a very common error.

2. The learner wrongly selects a continuous form to express a habit.

3. The learner is not aware that stative verbs, and particularly verbs expressing feelings or emotions, are not usually used in the continuous form unless a change of meaning is involved.

   cf. What *do* you *think* of the government? (Enquiry about general attitude) I *think* it's awful.

   but What are you *thinking* about? (Emphasis on process **at the moment**) I'm thinking about my girlfriend.

   Most grammars have lists of verbs of this type with notes on uses and restrictions.

4. The question *Will you go to the post office?* would be interpreted as a definite request, and sounds rather blunt and inappropriate here. The learner almost certainly intends to make a more neutral enquiry: *Will you be going to the post office?* (in the course of your visit to town); the future continuous in this type of context is seldom mastered even by the most advanced foreign learners as it is difficult to account for in structural terms.

5. The learner misunderstands the question as an enquiry about his reaction to the doorbell ringing. Again, a frequent mistake.

6. The learner has simply not internalised the fact that we use the simple past tense when talking about finished time; many other languages use the present perfect in such cases, making it doubly confusing.

7. A common misconception about the past perfect (here: *had built*) is that it is used to refer to the **very** distant past. In fact it is used to provide an extra dimension in the past (however recent or distant) when there is already one point of reference expressed by the simple past.

   e.g. *I had been asleep for quite a while when you* **came** *in.*

C. Many of these examples illustrate the confusion between tense and aspect which underlie the thinking of many learners – the present **continuous** (or progressive), for example is best thought of as an aspect of the present tense, not as a separate tense, especially since few other languages have corresponding verb forms and use adverbs or other means to express continuous aspect. It helps learners if the teacher stresses the conceptual links between continuous aspects of different tenses,

> e.g. **I'm working** *in London now.*
> *This time five years ago* **I was working** *in Paris.*
> *This time next year* **I'll be working** *in Rome.*

rather than dealing with each tense and aspect in isolation.

It is essential for teachers to familiarise themselves with the complexities of tense and aspect in a good grammar if they are not to confuse their learners.

SECTION EIGHTEEN

Commentary

A. 1. This is not true. The most obvious exceptions are:
I've just repaired the car (the action is complete).
I had only just repaired the car when it broke down again (past perfect used to express the time relationship between the repairing and the second breakdown).

In fact, the simple past tense is used when the time of an action is specified.

2. This is a half truth. It is certainly true to say that the present continuous form often occurs in statements about the future, but it does not itself express the future of
I'm watching T.V. and
I'm watching T.V. later this evening.
These continuous forms are identical; without a future time expression, the first example must be taken as referring to the present moment. In fact, the continuous form is almost certainly used more often in association with future meaning than as a description of an action in progress at the time of speaking.

3. This is an oversimplification based on grammars seeking to establish *shall/will* and infinitive as direct equivalents of future tenses in more highly inflected Latin based languages such as French and Spanish. Most people now

115

seem to agree that there is no single **future tense** in English, just a number of ways of referring to **future time.**

4. This is a very common misconception amongst foreign learners. The fact is that the past perfect may be used, if appropriate, about the very recent past as readily as about the distant past.

    e.g. She had already finished her supper when her parents came in. (could refer to almost any time).

5. This, too, is basically mistaken, and probably based on some concept of a sequence of tenses, appropriate to more rigidly *grammatical* languages.

B.
1. The present continuous tense is not normally used to express habits, but association with an adverb such as *always* or *continually* lends it this meaning, usually expressing a **persistent** habit.

2. The present simple seems out of place with the past adverb *yesterday* – this must be a caption under a newspaper photograph when such an apparently paradoxical association is possible.

3. The present simple expresses the immediacy of an action in a direct commentary on a sports event.

4. The present simple refers to the (future) departure time of a train or bus, possibly though not necessarily following a regular timetable.

5. Both tenses refer to the future, though the second verb is in the present simple because it follows the time conjunction *until.*

6. The present simple expresses a timeless scientific truth.

7. Past simple because the speaker knows Caruso to be dead.

8. Present perfect because the speaker knows Dylan to be alive and so may still go to one of his concerts.

9. Past simple because *(a)* Hemingway is dead, and *(b)* the writing of *The Old Man and the Sea* is clearly complete.

10. Dickens is dead, hence the past simple.

11. The writing of *The Power and the Glory* is complete, hence the past simple. The fact that Greene is still alive is irrelevant.

116

12. Present perfect because Heller is still alive and may write more novels.
13. This was a habit of Gladstone's during the known period of his lifetime (he is now dead) – this accounts for the use of *would*.
14. This, too, is a past habit. Compare:
    I smoke (present habit)
    and *I used to smoke* (discontinued habit)
    used to in this case supplies the true past of the present simple expressing habit.

C. 1. The learner has mistakenly assumed that the defective verb *used to*, with its clear past form, has a regular present form, as in the example.
2. Mistaken use of the simple present with the time expression *for six years*. In many languages (e.g. French and German), the present simple **is** used where we use the present perfect. The coverage of the concepts expressed by these tenses varies from one language to another.
3. Wrong use of simple past to express a (possibly) uncompleted action. (This usage is however common in American English).
4. Wrong use of present perfect with time adverb *yesterday* which clearly specifies the time of an action in the past, requiring the simple past.
5. Wrong use of past perfect based on the false assumption that this tense expresses events in the distant past.

D. There are enough clues to make each choice clear and unambiguous, but the six sentences are unconnected. There is no practice in context. The learner knows immediately what is required of him and will probably have little difficulty, on the evidence supplied, in getting these examples right, but will the learner be able to produce the appropriate verb forms in spontaneous speech when they are required? Text books abound with this type of exercise and yet mistakes are still made. Perhaps there is **overconcentration** on verb forms, resulting in a kind of verb neurosis in many learners.

E. (Other interpretations may be possible, depending on context)
1. Joe smokes heavily.
2. Keegan passes to Hughes.
3. Sugar dissolves in warm water.
4. The Carlisle bus arrives at noon.
5. Willy gets up at 7 every day.
6. Carter calls for energy summit.
7. Mary speaks fluent Spanish.
8. We'll phone you as soon as we get home.

A possible order of priority for teaching on a 'General English' course would be: 5, 1, 7, 8, 4, 3, 6, 2. 5 and 1 are conceptionally easy, most likely to correspond to usage in the learner's mother tongue, and are fairly frequently needed in *social* English.

SECTION NINETEEN

Commentary

A.
1. noun, noun
2. verb
3. verb, adjective
4. noun
5. noun
6. verb
7. adjective
8. verb
9. verb
10. verb, verb

The verbs and adjectives are all participles. The nouns are gerunds.

B. (Several alternatives suggested in each case; there are many more, of course.)
1. *silver/broken/new* (all adjectives)
2. *dull/acclaimed/good* (all adjectives)
3. my *dinner/the weekend/a quiet evening* (all nouns)
4. *fresh/frozen/delicious* (all adjectives)

5. *small meals/the dark/so much noise* (all nouns)
6. *that noise/the fight/work* (all nouns)

So, the . . . ing forms in 1, 2 and 4 are participles and in 3, 5 and 6 gerunds.

C.
1. The first example explains why he stopped whatever he was doing. The second one states what he stopped doing.
2. The first example is a reminder. The second asks whether the act can be recalled.
3. Both have the same meaning. The second example is more usual in American English.
4. The first example is a general enquiry. The second is an invitation.
5. The first example expresses the fact that she saw the whole action; the second states that she saw the burglar while he was climbing through the window though did not necessarily see the action from beginning to end.
6. The first example expresses the speaker's regret (retrospectively) at having told him. The second expresses regret felt at the time of speaking at having to break the bad news.

D. All of the errors have to do with inappropriate use of gerund (for infinitive) or infinitive (for gerund).
1. He has great difficulty in speaking English. *OR:* He finds it very difficult to speak English. (Error probably rooted in mother tongue).
2. I enjoyed visiting Cambridge yesterday. (Error probably results from false analogy or mother tongue interference).
3. He's going to bed late. *OR:* He used to go to bed late. (These two distinct forms are commonly confused, often as a result of contrastive teaching).
4. I'm looking forward to hearing from you. (The *to*, in fact a preposition here, has the unfortunate effect of **attracting** an incorrect infinitive).
5. He tried *to start* his car . . . (The change of **meaning** which results from the use of a gerund instead of an infinitive after *try* is not familiar to the speaker. *My watch has stopped. Try shaking it.* – the act is not

119

physically difficult – this is a **suggestion**; and *Try to concentrate* – make an effort).

6. I've always been interested in taking . . . (This indicates a general interest, such as a hobby; if I was interested *to read* the review of Greene's new book, this indicates a single occasion or focus of interest).

7. I don't feel like going . . . (false analogy or mother tongue interference).

8. I'm very pleased to see you (probably a straight confusion).

N.B.   Foreign learners find the **gerund vs. infinitive** problem extremely difficult. One reason is because textbooks often deal with it in a single chapter or unit and then regard it as *taught*. In fact, it is best dealt with as it arises, in context, and learners should be encouraged to note down whole constructions, including gerund or infinitive, and not just single words.

SECTION TWENTY

Commentary

A.   (Many variations possible.)
1. 'What colour is your pullover?'
2. 'What colour pullover do you want?'
    'Is that a blue pullover or a green one?'
3. 'Which pullover do you want?'
4. 'How does he drive?'
5. 'How often do you go dancing?'
6. 'Does he dance well or badly?'
7. 'What sort of a dancer is he?'
8. 'Where does he live?'

B.   1.   Two possible explanations. The utterance could read either:

Sally works hard.

or *Sally hardly works.*

If the former is intended, the speaker has wrongly assumed that *hardly* is the regular adverb form of *hard*.

120

If the second is intended, the mistake is one of word order.

2. Again two possible explanations. Either the mistake is one of word order. Corrected, this would become *My friend speaks English very well.* Or it is an adjective/ adverb confusion; the correct version would be *My friend speaks very good English.*

3. Probably false analogy with *How are you? I'm fine.* Corrected version: *What's the weather like?* (This could also be an error caused by interference from the mother tongue.)

4. May not be immediately perceived as an error. Learner has not grasped that *far*, whilst frequent in questions and negatives, is not usually used in straightforward statements of this sort. Corrected version: Aberdeen is a very long way from London.

5. Learner has not realised that *ill* cannot normally be used attributively (i.e. before the noun) with this meaning (i.e. sick). Corrected version: *I've just been to visit my sick friend.*

6. Incorrect use of adverb in a position normally occupied by an adjective. Corrected version: *That's not a very usual colour for a car.*

7. *Elder* used predicatively (i.e. after the verb to describe the subject); usually used only attributively. Corrected version: *My sister is older than I am.*

8. Incorrect adverbial formation. Adjectives already ending in *-ly* usually have a compound adverbial form e.g. *in a friendly way.*

C. 1. *Poorly* (an adjective meaning *unwell*) has the form (ending in *-ly*) which would normally identify it as an adverb. It also has an unexpected meaning.

2. Here, too, the form is that, apparently, of an adverb.

3, 4. *Hard* and *tight* are adverbs with a form indistinguishable from that of adjectives.

5. *Well*, normally an adverb, functions as an adjective here.

6. Elderly is an adjective with the form of an adverb.

D. 1*(a)* 2*(c)* 3*(d)* 4*(b)*.

too indicates an excess; *rather* indicates more than is really desirable; *quite* indicates a moderately positive reaction by the speaker.

SECTION TWENTY-ONE

Commentary

A.   1. Correct.
2. Incorrect. Commas must be deleted to make sense.
3. Correct.
4. Correct.
5. Incorrect. Commas needed before *which* and *but*.
6. Correct.
7. Correct.
8. Incorrect. Substitute *which* for *that*.
9. Incorrect. Delete comma.
10. Correct.
11. Incorrect. Comma needed before *who*.
12. Possibly acceptable, but certainly better with *who* substituted for *that*.

The commas are so important because they distinguish between a relative clause which **defines** and one which does not.

B.   A defining relative clause is an essential explanation which makes sense out of an utterance –
Child: The man hit me, mummy (inadequate information).
Mother: Which man? (Seeking essential closer identification).
Child: The one who sometimes comes to tea (Identifying more closely).

A non-defining relative clause adds extra, non-essential, information to an utterance. These clauses are fairly uncommon in spoken English as they render an utterance somewhat unwieldy. There is a tendency for sentences to be shorter and snappier in spoken English.

C. 1.⎤
    2.⎬ Because the relative clause is not so easy to identify in the
    3.⎦ absence of the relative pronoun. The sense may not be immediately clear.

    4. Because the relative pronoun refers to the whole preceding clause.

    5.⎤
    6.⎦ Again, no relative pronouns.

D. The prepositional phrases *in the red dress, on the hill above the village* and *by the door* all have similar force to relative clauses and could be expanded to be relative clauses:
    . . . who is wearing the red dress . . .
    . . . which is on the hill which is above the village . . .
    . . . which is by the door . . .

E. 1. Subject pronoun 'who' wrongly omitted. Learner may not realise that only object relative pronouns can be omitted.

    2. Student does not realise that *who* must be used for people and *which* for things.

    3. Student does not realise that *who* is the object of *spoke to* and feels the need for an object after the verb. A common mistake among Arabic and Farsi speakers.

    4. False analogy (preposition at end) with
    That's the house she lives in.

    5. *Whom* should be omitted. Student does not realise it is inappropriate in spoken English.

    6. Learner does not realise that *that* cannot always be substituted for *which*, and certainly not in relative clause referring back to the whole of the previous clause.

F. All are **cleft** type sentences in which a clause beginning with *it* or *what* precedes the main clause of the sentence, or in some cases (5 and 6) itself forms the subject of the following verb. In all of the examples a shift of emphasis is achieved.

    1. It was Clara . . . (not someone else!).

    2. It could have been Fred . . . (someone **did** ring; Fred is a possibility).

    3. . . . and not last Thursday or last Saturday.

    4. Emphasis on *Where* . . . would indicate that the questioner once knew but has forgotten.

5. Extra emphasis gained by introductory clause.
6. Whole clause **needed** here as subject of sentence.

Compare these less emphatic versions:
1. You saw Clara waiting at the corner.
2. Fred might have rung you up last night.
3. I first felt ill last Friday.
4. 'Where did you spend the weekend?'
5. 'We want Watney's.'
6. 'Your real beliefs are important.'

SECTION TWENTY-TWO

Commentary

A. All of them include inversions of subject and verb (either with or without an auxiliary).

B. 1. Normal interrogative formation – present simple tense.
2. Normal interrogative formation with modal auxiliary verb.
3. The position of *only* (at the beginning of the sentence for emphasis) requires inversion of subject and verb in the main clause.
4. The position of *hardly* at the beginning of the sentence provokes inversion of subject and verb. *Hardly* is one of a group of negative words and expressions (cf. also no. 9) which require this inversion when used to start a sentence.
5. A normal tail question (negative question tagged on to a statement).
6. Here, *Pop* is seen as an example of direct speech, and subject and verb are often inverted afterwards, cf., for analogy: *Hello, said John.*
7. Inversion is normal after demonstrative adverbs *here* and *there.*
8. Inversion after *so* is normal, though not obligatory. However, it is made more likely in this case because the subject, *all of us*, consists of more than one word.

9. The negative expression *Under no circumstances* at the beginning of the sentence requires subsequent inversion (cf. no. 4 above).
10. Inversion after *so* (cf. no. 8 above).
11. Normal inversion after *neither*.
12. Inversion here adds to the effect of a *live* commentary.
13. Inversion here replaces an *if* clause.

C. *Type 1* All of these are examples of inversion after **negative** expressions. The auxiliary *do (does)* is used in each case, as in the interrogative.

Type 2 In these examples, all in the present simple, there is straightforward transposition of subject and verb (for different reasons in each case), without an auxiliary.

D. x *Here my friend comes* (noun subject) would sound strange.

x *Here comes she* (pronoun subject) is not possible.

x *Up into the clear blue sky the bird soared* (noun subject) would be possible but less striking.

x *Up into the clear blue sky soared it* (pronoun subject) is not possible.

Pronouns do not admit inversion in such utterances.

E. 1. *Often* (adverb of frequency) should not usually immediately follow the verb it modifies. The most common correct version would be:
They often go to London.

2. *Marvellously* intrudes between the verb and its subject, which should normally not be separated. Corrected version:
My sister plays tennis marvellously.

3. The order of the adjectives is unlikely, if not incorrect. Depending on how closely the word *cuddly* defines *teddy*, a more acceptable version would be
... a new pink cuddly teddy ...

4. *Lend* is one of a group of verbs which can take both a direct and an indirect object. If the indirect object is a pronoun and the direct object is a noun, the following

word order applies:

Lend me your pen. (or *Lend your pen to me.*)

If both objects are nouns, the order is as follows:

He lent Jim ⎱ *his pen.* (or: *He lent his pen*
    the teacher ⎰   *to Jim.*)

If the direct object is a pronoun and the indirect object a noun, the word order required is:

He lent it to his teacher.

(Most grammar books supply a full list of verbs which can take both direct and indirect objects.)

5. The adverb *always* rarely starts a sentence. Corrected version:

    I always make that mistake.

6. Adjective *old* intrudes between the two parts of the noun group *man's coat*. The corrected version.

    That's an old man's coat.

    has two possible interpretations. Is it the man or the coat that is old? Reading aloud may help!

7. Theoretically, the word order is correct here. The speaker has learnt that a negative word at the beginning of a sentence requires subsequent inversion. He has, however, not learnt that such constructions are not appropriate to informal, everyday speech but are reserved for more formal spoken and written styles.

Unit Three

SECTION ONE

Commentary

A. 1) The important conclusion is that *pick* has many meanings and that some of them would not be relevant to learners of an intermediate level (e.g. as in sentences 2, 4, 5, 8, 9, 11 and 12). In addition, teaching a learner all the different meanings of *pick* at the same time would inevitably lead to confusion and to ineffective learning.

It is useful to decide that there are many different words which are spelled and pronounced *pick* and to teach only those which are likely to be useful to the learner. *Pick up*, as in sentence 1, is common and useful, as is *pick* in sentence 3 and *pick up* in sentence 7.

There is no one correct answer to the question of which *picks* to teach to an intermediate group; the important thing is that the teacher is selective and teaches only those *picks* which he thinks his learners should know.

In order to avoid the possibility of confusion it is better to teach the different selected *picks* at different times.

Most of the *pick* sentences in 1 would not be good teaching examples as in most cases the sentences do not provide very much information about the meanings of *pick* (e.g. sentence 2 and 11). New vocabulary items should be exemplified in contexts which help the learner to appreciate the meaning of the new item.

e.g. *Pick that glass up off the floor and put it on the table before somebody stands on it.*

2) Instead of referring the student to a dictionary the teacher should have referred him to the passage. The student's question makes it obvious that he does not realise that the item he does not know the meaning of is *pick up* and not *pick*. If he consults the dictionary he will find many meanings of *pick* listed and will have great difficulty in finding the one relevant to the passage. In

127

addition it is quite likely that he will not understand the definition even if he finds it.

Dictionaries can be an aid to vocabulary acquisition but only when the students have been taught how to use them and only if the students use them to check deductions they have made after analysing the form of the words and the contexts in which they have met them.

The teacher who persistently tells students to look words up in their dictionaries is encouraging the sort of painful intensive reading which consists of looking up every unfamiliar word regardless of its usefulness to the learner or its significance in the text.

3) Students should be discouraged from asking such questions and encouraged instead to pay more attention to the overall meaning of the text than to the exact meaning of every vocabulary item in it.

The question is best answered by saying that *pick* has many meanings and that the student should examine the passage he is reading to try to discover clues to the particular meaning of *pick* in the passage. The teacher should lead the student to discover that he is looking for the meaning of *pick up* in the text and to examine the previous and subsequent sentences for clues (such as the fact that the speaker has a car and that the two are going to travel in it together).

4) a) Only one of the definitions is relevant to the student's problem. The others are not only irrelevant but are meanings which are unlikely to be useful to an intermediate student even if he manages to learn them all without confusion.

b) Learning definitions does not magically bestow on the learner the ability to understand the word in context and does nothing at all to help him to be able to use it accurately and appropriately.

c) A learner could write five correct, *safe* sentences which tell the teacher nothing about the learner's ability to understand or use the item.
e.g. *Have you ever been to a port?*
I can see a port.

128

B. 1) The words in **heavy** type in each pair have the same referent; that is to say that they refer to the same thing. Thus *slim* and *skinny* refer to the physical characteristic of the same girl. However in each pair the words might have the same referent but they do not have exactly the same meaning. In each pair the two speakers have different attitudes to the same thing. Thus in 1 the first speaker does not like what Ali has become whereas the second speaker does; in 2 the first speaker finds Alice attractive whereas the second does not.

We can say that in each pair the words have the same referent but that they have different implied meanings.

2) a) The implied meanings of the words should be taught as well as their referents.

b) We should be very careful to distinguish between two items which are similar (but different) in meaning.

c) It can be useful to introduce a new item by relating it to a similar item which is familiar to the learners providing that attention is focussed on both the similarities and the differences.

C. 1) 1. *picture*
2. *shoes*
3. *pen*
4. *meat*
5. *seat*
   etc. etc.

2) a) When teaching beginners it is important to select items which have a high coverage; that is words which can be used by the beginner instead of other words. Thus *seat* can be used instead of *chair, sofa, bench* etc. and should thus be taught before them.

b) A word with high coverage is usually the most general item in a *family*. Thus *picture* is the most general item in the *family* which contains *photo, painting, drawing* etc. Advanced learners should be able to understand and use many of the particular items as well as the general item in each of the common word families in English.

129

When teaching a particular item from a 'family' it is important to focus attention not only on its membership of the 'family' but also on how it is different from the general item and from the other particular items in the family which have already been taught. Thus when teaching *bench* it is important to show that it is a particular type of *seat* and that the words cannot always be used interchangeably and to show how a *bench* is different from a *chair* and a *sofa*.

D. 1) In all the sentences the writer has used a word which has a meaning which is close to the one he wants to communicate but which for various reasons is not appropriate. Thus in 1 the writer has used *fracture* to mean *break* because he is unaware that *fracture* can only refer to the breaking of particular types of things (mainly bones). In 4 the writer has used *feeble* to mean *weak* because he is unaware that *feeble* is normally only used to refer to animate things (mainly people) which are weak.

Almost certainly the writer has made these errors because he has learned a new word as a synonym of one he already knows either as a result of consulting a dictionary, of incompletely deducing the meaning of a new word or of being taught that the new word = the known word. Thus the writer has learned that *manufacture* = *make* but has not learned that the two words are not always interchangeable because *manufacture* can normally only be used when things are made in bulk and made to be sold.

2) a) It is dangerous to teach or to imply that two words are synonyms (i.e. that their meanings are exactly the same).

b) It is important to teach when an item cannot be used as well as when it can be used. One way of achieving this is to teach the item together with known words which it is frequently used with (e.g. *eject from/ meeting*) and then to give examples of the types of words it cannot be used with (e.g. x *pierce/window* x).

130

Another way is to demonstrate the difference between the two related words (e.g. by contrasting pictures of people walking and people marching, and by asking questions about their purposes).

E. 1) The definitions consist only of equivalent words; they include no information about when it is appropriate to use the word being defined instead of its equivalent. For example, there is no information about when it would be appropriate to use *mate* (e.g. in informal conversation) and when it would not (e.g. in a formal interview).

2) The learner would probably think that the words were interchangeable and use those with restricted appropriacy (i.e. those being defined) in situations in which their use would be inappropriate (e.g. a worker addressing a letter requesting a rise to *The Boss*; someone starting a report, *Ten guys were selected for training*).

3) a) One word definitions are dangerous because they give the impression that the two words are interchangeable (i.e. that one can always be used instead of the other).

b) It is important to teach when it is appropriate to use an item and also to teach when it is not appropriate to use an item.

F. 1) a) Once two opposites have been taught it is often useful to indicate on a sloping line the relative positions of the items used to refer to degrees in between the opposites. This is particularly useful for example for showing that *quite good* is less than *good*.

b) Degrees in between opposites can be referred to by either:
a) adding another word to one of the opposites (*e.g. quite hot*)
b) using a different item (*e.g. warm*).
It is usually easier to teach *a)* first and then later to teach *b)*.

2) The same items can appear on two different lines of opposition. Thus *good* can appear on a line of ability as

well as on a line of virtue. It is important that the learner does not assume that the other items can appear on both lines, or he might, for example, use *poor* as an equivalent to *bad* on the line of virtue.

G. 1) *a)* In most contexts *reach* and *arrive* can have the same meaning and are equally acceptable. However, *reach* = *get in touch with* cannot be replaced by *arrive* and *reach out* = *stretch out* cannot be replaced by *arrive out*. *Reach* must always be followed by an object whereas *arrive* need not be. *Reach* cannot be used with *back* whereas *arrive* can. *Arrive* must be followed by *at* when its object noun is preceded by an article whereas *reach* is never followed by *at*.

    b) *Brave* and *courageous* appear to be interchangeable. However, whereas in many contexts *courage* seems to be able to replace *bravery, bravery* only seems to be able to replace *courage* when physical actions rather than mental actions are being referred to. In certain fixed phrases *bravery* can never be used instead of *courage*. There is no verb *to courage* corresponding to the verb *to brave*.

    c) *Put up* and *accommodate* seem to communicate the same meaning but *accommodate* is not normally used in informal conversation.

  2) To be totally interchangeable two words must be capable of always substituting for each other without changing the grammar, the meaning or the acceptability of the utterance.

  3) It is sometimes useful to introduce a new item by relating it to a similar item which is already known. However, it is very important to point out any potential differences in meaning, grammar or acceptability and learners should never be left with the impression that word *A* = word *B* (except for the few pairs which are totally interchangeable). It is also important to show that even if two words are apparently interchangeable their related forms might not be (*e.g. brave v. courageous; bravery v. courage*).

132

H. 1) It is important to realise that two words which are considered to be opposites will rarely be capable of a relationship of opposition in all conceivable contexts. If two words are introduced as opposites or if a new word is introduced as the opposite of a known word it is important to show when the two words are not opposites as well as when they are.

2) There is some point in teaching all these pairs together providing that initially the relationship of opposition is demonstrated in appropriate contexts, that the students never learn that word *A* = the opposite of word *B* and that eventually contexts are used to show when the two words are not opposites.

I. 1) *1* and *2* are useless teaching examples as in both cases the context gives no clue to the meaning of *amazed.* In *3 found out* gives some sort of clue to the meaning of *amazed* but it is not a very informative teaching example. *4* is a good teaching example as it contains a lot of information to help the learner work out the meaning of *amazed.* *5* gives clues to the unexpected aspect of *amazed* but is not a very good teaching example as it could give the misleading impression that *amazed* is always used to refer to unpleasant surprises *(cf. sentence 4).*

2) Such examples should be as informative as possible and ideally should enable the learner to accurately deduce the meaning of a word which is totally new to him.

J. The sentences tell you very little about the ability of your students to use *swept* as all the sentences are *safe* sentences which accurately imitate a model but do not contain any information which enables you to decide whether the student knows why or how you sweep a carpet.

Asking your students to write sentences using a particular word is basically a waste of time as very often correct sentences are produced which reveal nothing about the student's ability to understand and use the word. However, if such an exercise is set and safe answers are produced the

133

teacher can probe by asking such questions as 'Why did she sweep it?' and 'What did she sweep it with?'

K. *1.* i) 'nibbit' = biscuit (or possibly cake)

    Clues: a) *in your pocket* – therefore small and probably wrapped.

        b) *in case I was hungry* – therefore edible and probably more substantial than a sweet.

        c) *I prefer the ones with chocolate on*

        d) *That's probably why I didn't eat it*

   ii) 'slinned' = cleaned

    Clues: a) *took your coat to be . . .* – not done at home therefore probably done in a shop.

        b) *I hope they get all the stains out this time* – therefore definitely not *mended* or *altered* and almost certainly *cleaned* rather than *washed* (not normally done in shops or to coats anyway).

  2. 'ding' – slap

    Clues: a) *ding him* – therefore done to someone.

        b) *hard* – therefore physical.

        c) *He . . . naughty* – therefore a boy.

        d) *hurt* – confirms physical.

        e) *hand* – therefore not cane, ruler or fist.

        f) *on his leg* – therefore not *punch*.

        g) *soon get over it* – therefore not serious.

  3. i) 'glogget' – deckchair or folding chair

    Clues: a) *sitting in the garden*

        b) *didn't want it to get wet*

        c) *folded it up*

        d) *put it in the garage*

        e) *with the other garden seats*

   ii) 'unseddy' = untidy

    Clues: a) *I was furious*

        b) *I'd told the kids to put all their toys in the trunk to keep the garage seddy.*

        c) *there were toys all over the garage floor*

Learners can be taught to try to deduce the meaning of unfamiliar items from an analysis of the context.

L. 1) Various answers are possible. Our answers were:
- *1.* get something back
- *2.* a book with a card cover
- *3.* having too much of something
- *4.* below the moon
- *5.* twice a day
- *6.* like a punk
- *7.* i) think afterwards
- ii) the period after thinking
- *8.* make impossible
- *9.* i) recommend that something does not happen
- ii) withdraw a recommendation
- *10.* good at attending.

2)
- *1.* verb
- *2.* adjective or noun
- *3.* noun
- *4.* adjective
- *5.* adjective or adverb
- *6.* adverb
- *7.* verb or noun
- *8.* verb
- *9.* verb
- *10.* adjective

3) It is useful to teach students the meanings of common roots (e.g. *possib*) and prefixes (e.g. *post-*) and about how prefixes modify the meaning of roots. It is also useful to teach the grammatical and semantic functions of common suffixes (e.g. *-ate*).

Often a learner can work out the meaning of an unfamiliar word by examining the form and the context of the word.

M. 1)
- **?** It was sensational to hear.
- **?** It was amazing to eat.
- **x** It was superlative to eat/watch/hear/drive.
- **x** It was brilliant to eat/hear/drive.

2) All the words in column 2 could be used interchangeably in such a sentence as *It was a(n) – film*. However they are not always interchangeable. For instance it seems that *brilliant* when used in the pattern *It was + adj + infin* is

135

restricted to reference to *performances* and that *superlative* cannot be used in this pattern at all. It also seems that some of the adjectives in column *2* simply mean *very good (i.e. marvellous, superb and wonderful)* while others can sometimes mean 'very good' but can also have other meanings (e.g. *amazing* can mean *very good* or *very surprising*).

3) a) It is dangerous to assume that certain words are always interchangeable because they are interchangeable in a particular type of context.
    b) It can be useful to teach words in families providing that the grammatical and semantic sub-groupings are made evident.

N. 2) The words belong to the same family but are by no means interchangeable. Sub-groups can be formed on the basis of features of meaning. Thus sub-group *A1* might consist of *bought, purchased, hired, rented, borrowed, leased,* and *acquired* while sub-group *A2* consisted of *loaned, let, rented out, sold, leased* and *lent*. *A1* involves **movement towards** the subject. *A2* involves **movement away** from the subject. Another sub-grouping could be *B1 (bought, purchased, hired, rented, rented out, sold, leased, let)*, *B2 (borrowed, lent)* and *B3 (acquired, loaned)*. *B1* **includes** the payment of money, *B2* **excludes** the payment of money, and *B3* could either include or exclude the payment of money. Yet another sub-grouping could be *C1 (purchased, leased, acquired, loaned)* and *C2* (all other items). The items in *C1* are restricted in use in that they are normally only used in formal (and usually business) situations whereas the items in *C2* are not restricted in this way.

The words also differ in collocation (i.e. the words they can acceptably be used with). Thus *leased* is restricted in collocation to *house* and *business* and words like them. *Rented* can collocate with *house, car, business, tent, television* and words like them (i.e. words which refer to things you pay money for the continuous use of) and *hired* can collocate with such words as *house, car, business, tent, maid, television* and *picture* (i.e.

words referring to things or people you can pay to use for a short time). Another example of restricted collocation is the fact that *lent* cannot normally be followed immediately by *a* (e.g. x *I've lent a car*) whilst *acquired* cannot normally be followed immediately by *my* when it is preceded by the present perfect (e.g. x *I've acquired my business*). *Lent* could be said to belong to sub-group *D1* and acquired to *D2*.

O. This is a useful exercise for teaching the collocations of items in a *family* and thus for helping to teach the differences in meaning and use between the items.

It is important to realise that this exercise is only one stage in teaching learners to use the items accurately and appropriately as knowledge does not automatically lead to ability to use.

For a full treatment of these areas, see 'Teaching Vocabulary' by Michael Wallace (Heinemann, 1982).

SECTION TWO

Commentary

A. *Category one (verb + preposition): 4, 5, 7, 8.*
(prepositional verbs)

Category two (verb + adverbs) 1, 2, 3, 6, (phrasal verbs)

B. Each verb is followed by an adverbial particle and then a preposition.

C. 1. He'll have to be spoken **to** firmly (**to** is unstressed).
2. This work will have to be put **aside** (aside is stressed).
3. Three of the crew cannot be accounted **for** (**for** is unstressed).
4. The house was cleaned **up** after the party (**up** is stressed)
5. This form has been filled **in** (**in** is stressed)
6. A lot of ships have been laid **up** in the south-west of England (**up** is stressed).
7. The steelworks have been shut **down** (**down** is stressed).
8. This record has been worn **out** (**out** is stressed).

Foreign learners often find it difficult to distinguish between phrasal and prepositional verbs. This provides a useful test. Phrasal verbs (with adverb particles) carry stress on the adverb in the passive, and the adverb can be separated from the verb by its object – this applies to 2, 4, 5, 6, 7, 8 above. Prepositional verbs cannot be *split* and the preposition is unstressed in passive sentences. This applied to 1 and 3.

D.
1. **catch on** means understand. Not deducible from its parts.
2. **answer back** – the meaning can be deducted straightforwardly from the parts.
3. **gone off** – idiomatic meaning – not directly deducible.
4. **let down** – the meaning can be deducted from the parts.
5. **let down** – idiomatic meaning; not directly deducible.
6. **lay in** – idiomatic meaning; not directly deducible.
7. **run down** – idiomatic meaning; not directly deducible.
8. **put out** – idiomatic meaning; not directly deducible.
9. **stand up** – the meaning can be deduced from the parts.
10. **ran away** – the meaning can be deduced from the parts.
11. **knock off** – idiomatic meaning; not directly deducible.
12. **brush up** – idiomatic meaning; not directly deducible.

E. The exercise asks for phrasal verb synonyms for the Latin-based words in the exercise. It should be more useful if it gave some indication of when the Latinate equivalents are more appropriate (phrasal verbs tend to occur more in *informal* speech and writing). No reason is given for the substitution as an exercise.
The verbs required are:
1. taken out
2. brought up
3. looks like
4. put off
5. running . . . down
6. left out
7. gave . . . away
8. get away
9. died out
10. cut down

Note: Phrasal and prepositional verbs cause foreign learners a lot of difficulty, for reasons demonstrated in these exercises. They are best dealt with as items of vocabulary each time they appear, and learners should be encouraged to note down examples each time they meet a new verb of this type. R. A. Close in *A Reference Grammar for Students of English* (Longmans) offers a very full treatment of the subject, with useful categorisation, and there is a more exhaustive treatment in the *Oxford Dictionary of Current Idiomatic English* (Cowie and Mackin) Vol 1, which is devoted to phrasal and prepositional verbs.

The main structural teaching point is to give learners criteria for distinguishing between the types (see **B** and **C** above) so that they can handle the syntax.

Unit Four

SECTION ONE

Commentary

A. 1. Because it is not clear what the pronouns refer to. For example, what is **it** and who is **him** in sentence 1?

2. Either
   a) the pronouns rewritten as nouns
   or
   b) other utterances from the same conversations containing nouns referred to by the pronouns.

   e.g. *1. What's Bill's medicine doing here?*
   Have you given it to him yet?
   or
   c) information about the situations in which the utterances were made.

   e.g. *4. Two children are watching a film. They look bored. Mary points to the children and says, 'Have they seen it before?'*

3. Obviously there are many possible answers to this question. One possible answer is:
   1. Have you given your homework to the teacher yet?
   2. Are we seeing Bill and Mary again tonight?
   3. Did you buy your car from Joe Flynn?
   4. Have your children seen the film before?
   5. If I see Fred with Sophia again I'll tell you.
   6. Why did your daughter get angry?
   Her husband was very drunk.
   7. Sheila's dress is very beautiful.

4. If the nouns had not been recently referred to and if there was nothing in the situation which made it clear what or who was being referred to.

   e.g. *3. Two men are sitting in a pub discussing a second hand radio which one of them had bought from a local dealer. One of the men asked, 'Did you buy your car from Joe Flynn?' because he wanted to confirm that this was true before going on to compare the two second hand dealers.*

5. If the previous utterance(s) or something in the situation had made it absolutely clear what or who was being referred to.

    e.g. I get so envious of Sarah. My face is ugly. Look. Hers is beautiful.

6. Yes. For example, if the noun had already been mentioned by the speaker and the situation made it perfectly clear what was being referred to.

    e.g. 4. x Look at the children. <u>The children</u> seem bored by <u>this film</u>.

    Have <u>the children</u> seen <u>this film</u> before?

7. They are used to refer to people and things that have already been mentioned or are present in the situation. They help to avoid repeating expressions and stating the obvious and therefore contribute to the economy of utterances.

8. Because they refer to people who are present in the situation and therefore who do not need to be identified.

    They refer to participants in the conversation whereas the other pronouns usually refer to non-participants in the conversation and to people and things which are being identified either by reference back to what has been said or by *pointing* to them in the situation.

9. **her** is used to refer to a person whereas **hers** is used to refer to both the person and to something that belongs to her.

B. 1) *1. A* has wrongly assumed that *B* will know the place referred to by **there**.

   2. A has wrongly assumed that *B* will know the time referred to by **then**.

   3. A has wrongly assumed that B will know the things referred to by **those**.

   4. A has wrongly assumed that B will know the thing referred to by **that**.

   2) They refer to places, times or things which have previously been mentioned or which have been specified by the situation. They help to avoid repetition and to achieve economy.

3) 1. *they*
    2. *him*
    3. *then*
    4. *there*

A was right in assuming that *B* would perceive their referents (i.e. what they refer to) as a result of relating to previous mention or from pointers in the situation.

C. 1) Because the words with potential for breakdown in communication (i.e. *I, you, this, these, yours, here, now*) refer to referents present in the situation.

    2) All the words refer to referents which have previously been mentioned or are *pointed* to in the situation. However those in *1* refer to referents present and close in the situation whereas those in *2* refer to referents either distant from the speaker or not present in the situation at all.

D. 1. *B that* refers back to the vase.
        A that refers back to the breaking of the vase.
    2. *A this* refers back to the house.
        B this refers to what they are doing (i.e. to the situation).

E. 1. *a)* Could mean that the books were not the same as the two books previously referred to whereas *b)* could mean that the books were different from each other.

        In *a) different* refers you to previous utterances or to features of the situation to complete a contrast whereas in *b) different* acts as an adjective establishing a contrast between the two books mentioned in the utterance.

    2. *a)* I need some clothes in addition to these.
        b) I need some clothes instead of these.

Other warns you to refer to the situation and to previous utterances to help you decide whether it is being used with its function of addition or its function of replacement.

    3. *a)* *More* could refer back to a referent made clear by previous utterances or by the situation (e.g. more

potatoes) or it could be part of an expression indicating that the speaker thinks greater efforts are needed.

b) A realises that more people than expected have turned up to a function and says to *B We haven't done enough sandwiches. We'll have to do more.*
A is talking to *B* about a student who is not performing well and says, *We haven't done enough to help him. We'll have to do more.*

F. 1. They are all acting as substitutes for elements in previous utterances (e.g. in *1 one* is acting as a substitute for *cooker*).

2. a) substitutes for nouns
   b) substitutes for verbs
   c) substitutes for clauses
   d) substitutes for possessive pronoun plus noun.

G. 1. In all the utterances something has been omitted (e.g. *bought* in *1*).

2. *Group one (2, 3, 4, 7)* – nouns omitted.
   Group two (1, 5, 6, 8, 9) – verbs omitted.

3. a) Instead of repeating the same main verb in adjacent clauses or sentences you can often omit it in the second utterance.
   b) Instead of repeating the same auxiliary verbs in adjacent clauses or sentences you can often omit them (provided the main verbs are different and are included in the utterance).
   c) Instead of repeating the same subject in adjacent clauses or sentences you can often omit the subject in the second utterance.
   d) Instead of repeating the same object in adjacent clauses or sentences you can often omit the object in the second utterance.

H. *1.* All the sentences could indicate an equal liking for football and rugby but sentences 3, 4, 5, 6, 7 and 9 could indicate a preference for football whereas sentences 8 and 10 could indicate a preference for rugby. The actual interpretation would depend on the intonation of the speaker, the previous utterances and features of the situation.

2. *Type 1*
   and
   Joins two clauses within the same sentence; must come in between them.

   Type 2
   as well as; in addition to
   Joins two clauses within the same sentence; can come at the beginning of the first clause or in between the first and second.

   Type 3
   also; in addition
   Joins two sentences together.

3. 1, 2, 3 and 6 focus attention on the contrast between the expected and the actual performance of the car.
   4 and 5 focus attention on the fine performance of the car and then add the regrettable fact that it is old.

4. *Type 1*
   but

   Type 2
   although

   Type 3
   however

I. 2. *Type 1*
      and; also

      Type 2
      at the same time; then; so; as well as

      Type 3
      at the same time; then; all the other items in the list

3.

Exemplification	Sequence	Reason	Result	Purpose	Comparison
for instance	first	for this	as a result	for this	in the same way
for example	finally	reason	because of	purpose	likewise
thus		in that	this	with this	similarly
		case	thus	in mind	
		then	con-		
		so	sequently		
		on account	therefore		
		of this	then		
			so		

Addition	Contrast	Correction	Dismissal	Reinforce-ment	Time
and also	nevertheless	rather	anyhow	moreover	meanwhile
besides	even so	at least		in fact	at the same time
as well as	despite this	instead		as a matter	previously
	however	on the		of fact	finally
	on the other	other hand		in any case	
	hand			besides	
	on the			furthermore	
	contrary				

N.B. Some of the items could also belong to other categories e.g. *instead* could belong to *Replacement*.

3. Some of the differences are:
   a) Some of the expressions are used mainly in formal situations or in writing.
      e.g. *on account of this; for this purpose; thus; likewise; similarly; furthermore.*

   b) Some of the categories could be subdivided.
      e.g. *Contrast:*

Concession	Balance	Opposition
nevertheless	on the other	on the contrary
even so	hand	
despite this		
however		

   c) Some of the expressions are restricted as regards the linguistic environment they can be used in, e.g. *as a matter of fact* is normally used to reinforce a point following or in anticipation of an objection or challenge; *in that case* cannot be used with past reference.

J. 1. *Meanwhile* is normally used to indicate a connection in

145

time and in type between two events. Here it is only used to indicate a connection in time as a sinking and a heatwave are not connected in type.

2. *Nevertheless* suggests that something has just been referred to that might prevent enjoyment whereas the opposite is true.

3. *Anyhow* is not normally used to indicate resignation or concession; in this sentence it has been wrongly used instead of *however* or possibly *anyway*.

4. *On the contrary* is wrongly used. It is normally used to indicate contradiction in utterances in which *B* is the opposite of *A* and is substituted for it.

e.g. *Many people think that I'm going to resign. On the contrary, I'm going to work harder than ever before for the committee.*

In sentence 4 jazz and folk music are not opposites.

5. *In that case* is wrongly used with past reference. It is normally only used with future reference.

e.g. *A. It's just started to rain.*
B. In that case we'd better take our coats after all.

K. 1. *1.* plan; thing to do
   2. place
   3. stuff
   4. idea
   5. **thing**
   6. boy; lad
   7. woman
   8. creature

2. They are all lexical substitutes; that is they are all lexical items used to represent items previously used. They avoid repetition and in many cases indicate that the speaker has a negative attitude towards the referent.

e.g. *Put it away in that cupboard.*
Put the thing away in that cupboard.

In many of the sentences much stronger *negative* words could have been used than the ones chosen (*e.g. bitch in 7*).

L. It is important to teach the ways in which utterances are linked in English. If we do not our learners might understand the meaning of an utterance but not appreciate how it is connected with previous and subsequent utterances and they might be able to produce isolated utterances but not be able to produce continuous discourse.

It is important that the teacher understands the ways in which English achieves cohesion (i.e. the ways it uses to link various types of utterances) and that he makes use of this understanding in the planning of his teaching and practice material. It is particularly important that such material gives the learners the opportunity to respond to, participate in and produce extended and continuous discourse.

Unit Five

SECTION ONE

A.

		Type	Purpose
1.	A	Interrogative	Offer
	B	Declarative	Declining offer
	A	Declarative	Repeating and strengthening offer
	B	Declarative (negative)	Explaining the declining of the offer
2.	A*	Declarative plus interrogative	Seeking confirmation
	B	Declarative	Confirming
	A	Declarative	Statement of consequent action
	B	Interrogative	Polite request
3.	A	Declarative	Statement of fact plus criticism and indication of worry
	B	Imperative plus declarative	Reassurance
	A	Declarative	Criticism plus indication of worry
	B	Interrogative	Criticism plus indication of annoyance

N.B.* The above analysis reflects one valid interpretation. Other interpretations are possible (*e.g.* 2 *A** = *incentive to action*) as information about the relationship between the speakers, the setting of the dialogue, the shared knowledge of the speakers and the intonation pace and volume of the utterances is needed before a completely objective analysis can be attempted.

B. 1. 1) A wife is suggesting to her husband that he should cut the grass in their garden, as they are expecting visitors. The husband does not want to do it and reminds her that he is meeting someone soon and that he has been late for appointments with this person for the last two weeks.

2) A boy is driving his girlfriend home and suggests that they should stop for a drink at a pub. She is reluctant to stop and he tries to persuade her by suggesting that they might meet her friend.

3) A boy answers the phone and is mistaken for his brother. He tells the caller that his brother has left and suggests where he might be.

N.B. There are of course numerous other situations in which the exchanges would make sense.

2.

		Type	Purpose
1)	A	Declarative	Getting somebody to do something
	B	Declarative	Avoiding doing something
	A	Declarative	As A
	B	Declarative	As B
	A	Declarative	As A
	B	Declarative	As B
2)	A	Interrogative	Suggestion
	B	Declarative	Expressing reluctance
	A	Declarative plus interrogative	As A
	B	Declarative	As B
	A	Declarative plus interrogative	Persuasion
	B	Declarative	Indicating non-acceptance of suggestion in A
3)	A	Declarative	Greeting
	B	Interrogative	Seeking confirmation
	A	Declarative	Statement of information
	B	Declarative	Statement of information plus identification
	A	Interrogative	Expression of surprise plus annoyance
	B	Imperative	Suggestion

N.B. Other answers are of course possible.

3. a) It is important to make sure that the learner is not misled into thinking that declarative = statement,

149

interrogative = question and imperative = command.

b) The learner should be taught to participate in conversations in which the participants share knowledge and experience and therefore do not make the reference and purpose of every utterance explicit.

c) The learner should be taught how to effectively achieve his purpose through language (e.g. persuade someone to do something; turn down an invitation without giving offence).

d) Teaching the form and function of structures is not enough. We must also teach how to use them to achieve the purpose of an utterance (e.g. *My mother will be worried; will be* – prediction, but the whole utterance = reluctance to follow suggestion).

e) Learners should not be forced to use *full sentences* in dialogue practice.

C. 1. *1. Command*
   a) A in authority over B
   b) B accepts authority of A
   c) A wants B to do something
   d) B capable of doing what A wants

2. *Advice*
   a) B in need of help
   b) A accepts that B needs help
   c) A in position to help
   d) B accepts that A in position to help
   e) A does not intend to do anything but intends B to do something

3. *Appeal*
   a) A in great need of help
   b) help previously asked for
   c) B in position to help A

4. *Instruction*
   a) A has greater knowledge, expertise or experience than B
   b) B accepts a)
   c) B needs A to tell him what to do

150

   5. *Warning*
      a) B in *danger*
      b) A informing B of *danger*
      c) B capable of averting *danger*
      d) A knows how B can avert *danger*
2. Listing conditions as above can help the teacher to devise situations which will help the learner to appreciate the difference between similar potential functions of the same utterance (e.g. teacher-pupil in science laboratory for *instruction* and father-young son at home for *command*).

D. 1. Criticism through prediction of consequences.
   2. Exemplification to reinforce criticism.
   3. 'all industries should be nationalised' and 'let us encourage private enterprise'
   4. When private enterprise has been encouraged?
   5. To link 'prosperity' to 'initiative' as its consequence.
   6. a) Criticism
      b) Prediction
      c) Exemplification
      d) Exemplification
      e) Refutation
      f) Suggestion
      g) Reinforcement of suggestion

E. 1. *No tapes for the winter term*. Because the *answer* refers to tapes.
   2. The lack of money as a result of the spending of the budget.
   3. *We have a problem*, and *I think I've got an answer*.
   4. The use of *that* in *that spare set of Mullens*, implies that the addressee is aware of these books and is therefore working at the school. The *of course* in, *That means of course no tapes* also suggests that the addressee works at the school and therefore that the *we* includes the addressee.
   5. Books. Because of *set* and because 'Mullens' is in inverted commas.

151

6. It is important to teach how to detect and make links between consecutive and between separated utterances.

F. 1. *Furthermore* is normally used to introduce an additional point which reinforces the similar ones already made. In this text it does not seem to have any such semantic function.

2. There is no logical link between sentences 3 and 4 because of the differences in tense.

3. *Another factor* does not logically link its utterance to any previous utterance. Another factor in what?

4. *Especially* does not logically link its utterance to the previous one.

5. Does sentence 6 refer to the electrification of motor vehicles?

6. *However* does not logically link its utterance to the previous one.

7. *As a result* does not logically link its utterance to the previous one.

8. There are no grammatical or vocabulary errors in these two paragraphs but the writer's inability to link his utterances logically makes them very difficult to understand.

Unit Six

SECTION ONE

Commentary

A. 1. 1. **fisherman**
    a) False analogy with baker, farmer etc.
    b) Overgeneralisation that in English agent nouns are formed by adding -er to the simple form of the verb.

  2. **can see**
    a) Overgeneralisation that the present continuous is always used when reference is being made to a continuous action in the present.
    b) Overteaching/overlearning of the present continuous as a result of intensive drilling of the tense in association with *now* situations.
    c) Chronology – i.e. the tense was the first learned and is now dominant.

  3. **likes**
    a) Overgeneralisation that the present simple has the same form as the infinitive.
    b) Perception of the redundancy of the *s* (i.e. it is not essential for effective communication).

  4. **lives**
    a) Failure to discriminate between the sound /i/ (in *lives*) and /i:/ (in *leaves*) leading to a spelling confusion.

  5. **I go**
    a) Overgeneralisation that the future can always be referred to using *will.*
    b) Ignorance of the rule governing time clauses with future reference in English.
    c) Failure to appreciate that *will* is not a tense but a modal indicating either willingness or a present decision about the future.

  6. **isn't she?**
    a) Interference from a mother tongue which has a fixed question tag form (*e.g. 'n'est-ce pas?'*).

153

b) Ignorance of the *rules* of question tag formation in English.

7. **went**
   a) Failure to distinguish between the present perfect = indefinite past and the simple past = definite past.
   b) L1 interference (i.e. interference from a mother tongue which does not make the distinction between definite and indefinite past).
   c) Overlearning of present perfect = recent past.

8. **lend**
   a) L1 interference (i.e. from a language which has the same lexical item as the equivalent of both *lend* and *borrow*).
   b) confusion from learning both items at the same time.

9. **has stolen**
   a) L1 interference (i.e. from a language that has the same lexical item as the equivalent of both *steal* and *rob*).
   b) confusion from learning both items at the same time.

10. **so that I could book**
    a) Confusion with so + V = result.

11. **went**
    a) Failure to distinguish between the past perfect = first of two or more past actions and the simple past = specific action in the past.
    b) Overlearning of the past perfect (especially by student whose L1 does not have an equivalent of the English past perfect).

12. **injured**
    a) Overgeneralisation of the reference of *wounded.*
    b) L1 interference (i.e. from a language which has one lexical item as the equivalent of both *wound* and *injure*).

13. **he had asked**
    a) Ignorance of the tense sequence of the Third Conditional.

b) Interference from strong association between the simple past and events in the past.

14. **a friend came**
    a) Interference from L1.

15. **too**
    a) Failure to perceive the different roles of *too* and *to*.
    b) Pronouncing *to* as *too* (even when the vowel of *to* should be weakened as a result of lack of stress) and thereby adding to the confusion between the two words.

16. **We couldn't care less**
    a) L1 interference.
    b) Confusion as a result of learning many English idioms.

17. **to swim/for a swim**
    a) L1 interference.
    b) Overgeneralisation for + V-ing = purpose of instrument (e.g. It's for cutting wood).

18. **My mother is**
    a) L1 interference from a mother tongue which uses personal pronouns to repeat subjects.

19. **she**
    a) L1 interference from a mother tongue which does not differentiate between male and female in its system of personal pronouns.

20. **playing**
    a) Overgeneralisation of S + V + V infinitive.

2. 1. L1 interference.
    2. False analogy.
    3. Overgeneralisation.
    4. Overlearning.
    5. Ignorance.
    6. Incomplete learning.
    7. Interference from other items in English.

B. 1. *1.* I will be a football player.
       2. when I will be back
       3. to my home

     4. I will be professor
     5. in school
     6. what for?
     7. will enjoy
     8. be teach
     9. is bore
   10. will be interest
   11. it will be rich
   12. professor will be rich
   13. not true
   14. football player
   15. very much rich
   16. football player
   17. not be rich
   18. not give
   19. he will be give
   20. lot of money

2.   *1.* I am going to be a footballer
     2. when I go back/return
     3. home
     4. I am going to be a teacher
     5. in a school
     6. why?
     7. will enjoy it
     8. be a teacher
     9. is boring
   10. is more interesting
   11. will make me rich
   12. a teacher is well paid too
   13. that's not true
   14. a footballer
   15. is much richer/much better paid
   16. a footballer
   17. is not rich/well paid
   18. is not given much money
   19. he is given
   20. a lot of money

3.   1. **x** be a football player
         1. no system of articles in L1

2. false analogy of football player with tennis player etc.
3. literal translation of football player from L1 equivalent

2. **x** be professor
   1. no system of articles in L1
   2. L1 interference

3. **x** will enjoy
   1. confusion between transitive and intransitive verbs
   2. L1 interference from intransitive
      transitive equivalent of *enjoy*

4. The learners have made many errors because they have attempted a *free* conversation at an elementary stage of learning and have therefore inevitably made errors caused by ignorance, L1 interference, false analogy and over-generalisation. However the two learners have basically managed to communicate and it would be a mistake for the teacher to draw attention to all their errors. This would negate the important feeling of successful communication, would discourage and probably inhibit the learners and would impose far too great a load of re-learning for it to be of any remedial value. It would be much more useful to focus attention on errors which the two learners both frequently make (e.g. the omission of the indefinite article) and on errors which could cause misunderstanding (e.g. *professor* for *teacher*, *not give* for *is not given*).

C. 1. In the first extract the learner has got the past simple tense of the three irregular verbs right but has omitted necessary articles and the pronoun object of *read*. In the second extract he has used articles and a pronoun object correctly but he has got the past simple tense of the three irregular verbs wrong.

2. In the two weeks he has obviously learned how to use the indefinite article and the pronoun as object. However it also seems that he has *strongly* learned the regular form of the simple past tense (i.e. V + -ed) and that over-

generalisation of this form has caused him to get wrong what he got right before.

D. The learner can use the correct form of the third person of the simple present tense (i.e. *lives, cycles, goes, plays, comes*) but gets it wrong after a conjunction (i.e. after *but* and *and*). This suggests that he has problems with coordination rather than with the present simple tense.

The learner also uses connectors (i.e. *however* and *nevertheless*) as though they were link words. That is he uses them to join two clauses within a sentence rather than to join two sentences together.

E. 1.

	Error	Correction
1.	to my bed	to bed
2.	there came a friend	a friend came
3.	died	had died
4.	to meet	meeting
5.	when there were stairs	when we came to some stairs
6.	upstairs	up them
7.	his shin	whose skin
8.	a scarp	a scar
9.	in his face	on his face
10.	beconed	beckoned
11.	in my back	behind me
12.	holding a gun	holding guns
13.	I went near	I moved near to the man
14.	, the man had . . .	He had . . .
15.	died	had died
16.	from an accident	in an accident
17.	I said I could manage it, so he got a lot of money	I said I could arrange it so that he got a lot of money
18.	He would gave	He would give
19.	to do everything in order	to arrange everything
20.	tied on a chair	tied to a chair
21.	We made up a story	We devised a plan
22.	back, they	back. They

23.	He took	The man took
24.	took his knife to my heart	pointed his knife at my heart
25.	want to come near with his knife	tried to attack me with his knife
26.	asked what there was happened	asked what had happened
27.	happened I said	happened. I said

2. *Types of Error*
   1. *Tense Errors*
      Failure to use past perfect when required
   2. *Prepositional Errors*
      Use of wrong prepositions (especially after verbs)
   3. *Adverbial Errors*
      Problems expressing the concept of relative position
   4. *Word order*
      Subject placed after verb
   5. *Punctuation*
      a) Comma instead of full stop
      b) Comma when not required
   6. *Spelling*
   7. *Lexical Errors*
      Most of the errors are in this category.
   8. *Underuse of connectors*
      Most of the sentences start with personal pronouns and therefore the logical link between sentences is not always clear.

Possible Causes of Error
   1. *L1 interference*
      a) Direct translation (e.g. . . . *there came a friend to me . . .*).
      b) Interference from L1 construction (e.g. . . . *would gave me three hours to do everything in order*).
   2. *Overlearning*
      Simple past always used to make past reference.
   3. Interference from similar English expression, e.g.

shin (skin); *scarp* (scar); *could manage it, so he got a lot of money* (managed it, so he got a lot of money).

4. *Ignorance*
e.g. complete inability to manage reported speech of past perfect passive (x *she asked me what there was happened*).

5. Using the known for the unknown – e.g. *story* for *plan*.

F. 1.

Error	Correction
1. In a little local village	In a little village
2. switched on television	switched on his/the television
3. had been broken down	was broken
4. to get a ladder	so he could use it
5. to fix it	to fix the aerial
6. so he had to shout	so he shouted
7. on earth again	back to the ground
8. at home	in the house
9. switched on television	switched on the television

2. *3, 5, 7.*

G. 1.

Error	Correction
1. has been taken	had been taken
2. but	and
3. in hospital	in the hospital
4. must	had to
5. after closing time	after visiting time was over
6. lonely	alone
7. granted him permission	allowed
8. shortly	for a short time
9. If he told me he was going	If he had told me he was going
10. I could give him a lift	I could have given him a lift
11. would have	could have

2. *1.* *lonely* for *alone* or *closing time* for *after visiting time was over*

2. *granted him permission*

160

3. *shortly* for *a short time*
4. *in hospital* for *in the hospital*
5. *He has been taken*

Index

1 The references are to units, sections, exercises and example numbers
   e.g. *Opposites* 3.1.F, H.
                    Unit 3, Section 1, Exercises F and H
2 Reference can be made to both the exercises and the commentaries
   using this system.
3 References in **heavy** type indicate that the topic is given thorough
   treatment, or that the whole exercise or section is devoted to it.
4 Grammatical terms and notions are printed in ordinary type.
   Individual words dealt with from a grammatical point of view are
   printed in *italic*.

163